SECRETS *of the* CONSTRUCTION INDUSTRY

THE MOST IMPORTANT INDUSTRY PRINCIPLES REVEALED

ELINOR MOSHE

IN A PREMIERE COLLABORATIVE ANTHOLOGY

Cover design by: Ida Jansson

Typeset by: Dylan Ingram

Edited by: Chelsea Wilcox

Proofread by: Eleanor Narey

Typeset in Adobe Garamond Pro 12.5/18pt

 A catalogue record for this work is available from the National Library of Australia

National Library of Australia Catalogue-in-Publication data:

Secrets of the Construction Industry / Elinor Moshe

ISBN: 978-0-6468872-4-1

'The lips of wisdom are closed, except to the ears of understanding.' – The Kybalion

CONTENTS

PREFACE

BY BEN SHADDAI MOSHE

Principles are extremely important guiding lights in life. Without solid principles, a person is only relying on their ego which will only lead them astray and into a fear-based way of living. Principles alone can be our shared truth, which allows one a greater baseline of making great decisions when it comes to their career and life. Principles have also brought on great success in my life, as I have chosen to selectively follow the truth they provide. I was born in Iraq, working to sell matches for ten cents a day to ensure food was provided for my family of eight siblings, and it is wisdom that has allowed me to rise – mentally, spiritually, financially, emotionally, physically. I consider myself deeply blessed, because I searched for knowledge and wisdom all my life, as I hope you are now too.

I have spent years in deep study and introspection discovering the words of great philosophers and guiding truths to lead a life embedded in deep faith and servitude to the creator. When my daughter said she was collating a principle-based book, sharing profound wisdom of advanced minds, I felt drawn to sharing the life lessons, powerful quotes and principles to you as well. In sharing my life guiding principles, I hope you find success on your own terms and life guided by your highest truth and purpose. Each of these, I have lived by, and in doing so, have been able to redirect my destiny to my own highest good, instead of falling for the ego of others.

As you absorb these principles, consider it the priming of your mind to receive great wisdom that is embedded to guide you in the pages that come after this. So, without any further ado, here are my twenty important guiding principles and quotes that I am honoured to share with you:

1. Obsession based in fear is very negative and it's seen in the everyday of most people's life. The very thing we obsess about with fear, even if you truly desire it, is only putting the brakes on it.

2. The power to say 'no' is critical. It is the word that saves us many troubles if used in the right moment. Sometimes, we feel guilty when we say it. Beware – this is the trick of the 'ego'.

3. We achieve things in life, but where does the credit go? We take the credit for ourselves, but this is wrong. The credit should always be given to our creator, or the great that is within you, which is always there to guide us in every moment of our life.

4. Go and tell no-one. This is a very important thing. We should remember that sometimes we feel the need to tell

our secrets and plans, but it ends up being to the wrong person, and we regret this.

5. Do not be a guarantor for anyone unless you can pay whatever you sign. You will fall in a hole if you blindly sign anything for anyone out of sheer goodwill.

6. Reliving the past in our memory is like saying that a grain of salt on our back is weighing us down. Trying to relive the past is like chasing the wind. Let it go, where it's not serving you.

7. Worry not about the result, for the very thing we worry about is what we cannot control.

8. Prejudice in the mind doesn't serve you or others. The people who carry prejudice are only hurting themselves.

9. Every person you meet in your life is someone you can learn from. Even the fool, for it will show you what not to do. Even the wise, for it will show you what to do.

10. Live amongst people like God is with you.

11. To understand something and then choose to not to do it is because of a lack of courage.

12. Confucious said, before you complain how much snow there is on the roof of your neighbour, see how much snow there is on your roof.

13. Only noble friends will be happy about your achievements.

14. The brave person moulds his life, and the diligent hand brings prosperity.

15. If you believe that you can achieve something, you will have the power to do it.

16. Friendships with bad people destroy good character and waste your time.

17. When a great man appears in the world, you can recognise him, because all the fools in the world rise against him.
18. God doesn't help the lazy.
19. Do your work faithfully and let others criticise you, for it's not a reflection of you, but them.
20. A noble person looks within himself, the inferior looks to others.

Shall this meet you at the right time and when you need, and shall you seek to fill your mind with wisdom as your guide for your path in this life. Believe in yourself, all the help that you need is within you. Seek to do the best you can in your life, so that even more greatness can come into your life. I wish you all the best.

Ben Shaddai Moshe

INTRODUCTION

What is one thing you would tell a person?

Imagine that someone not in this world or of this world were to find themselves in this game called life and ended up in the construction industry. And they were only able to receive one piece of wisdom, knowledge or critical advice. On that one foundational piece of advice, they'll build everything. Receiving the wrong advice from the outset, well, you work in the industry so you can envisage what happens thereafter; it's a tower that will collapse without fail. Being personally and professionally misled has severe and dire consequences, which after being the industry for a decade, I see as the status quo, and it's not working. Yet, few have stopped to ask why isn't it working?

If the general advice that was being given through mainstream platforms was working or beneficial to the rising of the collective, we would see more success stories and less statistics. More enlivened and inspired people than burnt-out and one-dimensional professionals. Most of the advice propagated is, to certain extents, myriad with misinformation, disinformation, parroted mainstream advice, tactical advice, biased advice and plain old irrelevant, outdated advice. And it's typically this advice that's perpetrated and propelled by those with little to no results for themselves. So, then we have those that come after attempting to build themselves in this industry on weak foundations. Why? Because everyone else is doing it, so it must be right. How can 90% of people have it wrong and so backwards? Well, history has always proven that majority are wrong. It's like trying to place a steel structure on sand foundations. It's bound to topple. Again, few stop in their tracks to question this, first and foremost for themselves. Ask, *How is it that 90% of people around me, year after year, are nowhere and simply haven't grown?*

Yet, despite all the access to information in the industry, who is truly better off and wiser for it? Have you noticed how many mainstream narratives have been pushing the same agenda for years, yet nothing of merit or real structural value has taken place? Have you ever questioned this? As I have been questioning and seeing cracks in what was once a solid formation for many years, I realised there's a stark omission in the industry. Societally speaking too. And it's wisdom. It's the *truth*.

You see, wisdom is so simple, dense, elegant, beautiful, paradigm-shifting, mind-bending, all at once. Wisdom cuts through the noise. It's a thousand chapters condensed into one sentence. Wisdom is how knowledge has withstood the test of time, for its simplicity and density combined. Wisdom is irrefutable, for it's an expression of the truth, and truth doesn't have multiple interpretations. However, it's easy to say what you want to say in ten thousand words, but have you tried saying it so perfectly in one sentence? In a way that it simply lodges into the mind of the reader and makes more sense to them than anything else? Wisdom simply refers to embodied experience. This is to translate the experience into a lesson. Wisdom is not theory. You can intellectually understand something, but to play it out in reality is a whole other realm of character and competence. It's why some people are wise and some are simply not.

And the return to wisdom is what significantly changed my whole life, especially over the recent years when there was immense inner and outer turbulence. Only in wisdom could I anchor myself. Only timeless truths were my guiding light in a storm that felt fierce at times, and as I write, is still happening on different levels. And it's why I had to bring the collective wisdom to you, in your hands, to your mind. Because there's too much out there – online and offline – that simply doesn't work, and time has proven it. And by the time you figure that out, you've probably been misled, and even worse, wasted your time! Do you have time to read all the books and listen to all the podcasts? No, certainly not. And in the interim, you think you're building a concrete foundation for yourself in the industry – alas, it's a mere bed of sand.

It's this which served as the impetus to creating this one-of-a-kind anthology, an exposé and compilation of the wisdom that can be found in the industry. It's there. Except wisdom whispers, so softly heard, but those who have tuned in to hear it, will. Now you have access to it. You can see what works, from those who have the battle scars of experience and trial by fire to know what truly works and what doesn't.

When I embarked on my fourth book, I wanted to bring in a global choir of voices, so that the whisper of wisdom can reach more corners of the industry laden in darkness. Reading this book is a pick-your-own-adventure type read. Some principles may not hold immediate relevance to you, but if you are not seeding new knowledge today, what will you have to harvest in years to come when you need it the most? Other principles will serve as the exact guidance you need for your qualms and quandaries right now. However, the differentiating factor is always what you will do with this new-found wisdom. Act or stay the same? Beware of your own narrative that kicks in. You may be thinking, *Well, I've heard this before.* If so, what have you done with it? How have you sought to improve yourself because you have heard something? Beware of the illusion of knowledge, for that is not the language of the wise.

At the same time, to get the most value from the book, will you be required to engage in self-reflection. This may be your hardest task yet, as looking within is where you may not be accustomed to looking. Holding yourself accountable to live by principles is an attribute of a person with remarkable character. Most people live their life off erroneous beliefs that aren't serving them. I can only encourage you to revisit the chapters again and again in reflection and contemplation. I can only encourage you to read this book slowly and consider after each chapter how you will implement the new-found wisdom in your life. It's wisdom itself to know when to translate knowledge into action.

Each chapter that you will discover hereon is a response to the signature question presented to each co-author: 'What is one thing you would tell a person?' *Why this question?* you ask. I want to get an excavator and smash the surface straight into the depth of a person. What do they live by? I don't care about the titles, the project values and technical skill set. I care about what's in one's heart. The lessons learnt the hard way. I care about what they have to say to those who are coming after them. I care about the wisdom being captured, that the next generation only knows the best of the best. Shall anything lesser than be washed away with time, but the moments in time which defined a person captured. I want the wise to have their name live on, that our industry shall not forget those who had a great heart and mind and the energy to lift up those around them. Shall their names live on long after the project is completed. Shall the bright minds of the industry have a space to capture their decades of experiences and battle scars. Shall all the wars fought not have been in vain, and each scar that we carry tell a story for those after us. The real industry genius is cemented, shared with minds who will contribute to the collective betterment of the industry.

I purposely left the question open-ended, and without ruining the surprise, the most important thing that exemplary leaders, industry titans and young guns have to tell you has nothing to do with your technical skill set. Not even a percentage is mentioned as such, yet more and more professionals run for certifications, licences and degrees, thinking that's what will enable them to win. Do you *really* not want to win, that you'll do what others are doing like it's 1965? Those who seek the path of the masses will always be misled. Whatever the path drove you here to seek, I hope you find. As do I hope that this is only the start of your journey to seeking wisdom and listening to the wisdom that is already within.

Before you discover the first principle, I would like to send a heartfelt thank you and deep appreciation for each co-author that decided to believe in the mission of wisdom transference to change the tide of the industry. For their belief in the collective exchange of wisdom for the upheaval of archaic and stale belief systems. For their time in deep consideration and contribution to deliver their masterstroke to you with such concision and precision. I hope you use this book as a torch to shed more light into your mind so that you too can win at whatever path you seek for yourself.

Ready?

Author's note: The views of each co-author are not reflective of the views of another. Each co-author has expressed their truth from their experiences. Any of the views or content are equally not endorsed by Elinor Moshe. The nature of any work, business or function of a co-author outside of their contribution to Secrets of the Construction Industry is also in no affiliation or correlation to The Construction Coach or with any other co-author. All biographies are correct at the time of printing.

I had the pleasure of connecting with Igbuan Okaisabor's team during the writing process, who shared their experience of him as a leader. Thirty years on from the conception of the original vision, he still, full of heart, sees every opportunity to engage and instil the Construction Kaiser Limited vision into everyone he meets. Imagine speaking into reality your vision for decades without a diminishing rate of enthusiasm and captivating the hearts and minds to collectively create such a positive transformation in a socio-economic and politically challenged field. What's the driving principle behind this exemplary leader? Let's discover his secret now.

1
SECRETS OF CONSTRUCTION SUCCESS

BY IGBUAN OKAISABOR

WHAT IS ONE THING YOU WOULD TELL A PERSON?

The only way to translate a vision into reality is to broadcast it and align it with the right people.

WHY?

In the realm of true leadership, a clear and compelling vision is paramount. However, a vision is only as good as those who buy into it. It is important for a leader to rally both internal and external stakeholders around a common path to achieving the vision. For this, a leader needs to actively invest in fostering strong relationships and lead with empathy. The ability to lead with empathy is a defining trait, demanding a deep understanding of others' perspectives and intricacies. By intertwining vision, persuasion and empathy, a true leader creates an environment where collective aspirations are pursued and attained harmoniously.

THE BIRTH OF CONSTRUCTION KAISER LIMITED (CKL)

In 1992, while walking through the driveway of the Michelin factory in Port Harcourt, I saw an expatriate giving orders to Nigerian workers on a project. It was at that point I wondered why we could not have indigenous construction companies operating to high standards in Nigeria. This made me think, *What if we started a construction company maintaining quality while reducing overhead costs related to expatriates?* This was the beginning of Construction Kaiser Limited in 1993, with just five of us working from my living room in Rumuogba, Port Harcourt. Today, we are moving forward with almost 150 workers executing construction projects in heavy engineering, residential and commercial development across different geopolitical zones in Nigeria. This journey stands as a testament to the resilience of a shared dream.

PERSUASION AND BUILDING RELATIONSHIPS

Persuasion was the first crucial cornerstone in bringing the vision to life. Getting people to agree with the CKL idea was essential. I believed in our vision: to be an innovative, solution-driven and value-creating indigenous construction service provider guided by the highest quality standards. I worked to get others onboard, even though it was uncommon in the context of business typically carried out in Nigeria.

Building strong relationships is always a priority for CKL. We have realised that 80% of our success has come from our relationships, while 20% is attributable to product knowledge, which is the second cornerstone of ensuring the vision lives on.

LEADERSHIP AND COMMUNICATION

'Leadership is not about titles, positions or flow charts. It is about one life influencing another.' – John C Maxwell

To build and nurture genuine relationships, real communication is required. Real communication means mutual understanding, and titles don't matter as much as the positive influence one exerts on another. To communicate and influence positively, a true leader must be knowledgeable and cross-functional. Understanding different aspects of business is crucial. Even as a civil engineer, I consistently made an effort to have one-on-one conversations with my team members from finance to QS professionals. While it may not be in-depth, understanding their roles has allowed for effective communication and collaboration. A leader must have a broad understanding across all spheres. I dedicate my time to learning about everything from politics to numbers and even current affairs. I do not have to know everything in detail, but learning a bit about everything helps to build good conversations leading to better relationships and trust with clients and my team to foster a better working environment and ultimately influence people to carry on with the vision even when you are not there.

LEADING WITH EMPATHY

'People work for people, not companies.' – Gerard R Griffin

I have recognised that people work for people, not just companies. Treating employees with respect and showing them that their opinions matter is a priority. Being a good listener and valuing the input and expertise of others creates an environment where people feel valued and motivated to achieve the vision. Many times, at meetings, I am always the last to speak because I believe it is important to give people the opportunity to add value as a member of the team.

'Leaders eat last.' – Simon Sinek

Leading with empathy is the third cornerstone to sustaining a vision. In leading with empathy, servant leadership is key. It is crucial for a leader to prioritise his team. Beyond work, we make an effort at CKL to care about our employees as individuals. During the challenging times of the COVID-19 pandemic, we had workers working on projects in remote areas. We made it our duty to check on their wellbeing and support their families. Building trust and showing genuine care has been instrumental in retaining both clients and talented individuals within our organisation. However, while leading with empathy has been integral to my leadership style, I have learned that to build a sustainable business, it is crucial to separate your personality from your job. A leader's personality can affect them positively and negatively. Many entrepreneurs are shrewd, but in addition, I am empathetic and emotional. I remember my parents telling me, as a young man leaving home from the National Youth Service Corps, that I should be mindful of the fact that many people do not have a heart like I do. To this day, I still have similar types of conversations with my children because of my personality. Sometimes, being a leader means making hard choices, like the times we have had to let some people go. It was tough, but clarity in achieving the vision, building a sustainable business and values helped us make those decisions and stay true to what we believe in.

BUILDING ON INTEGRITY

One of my core values is integrity. I firmly believe in operating ethically and refusing to engage in corrupt practices, and this has been instilled in the way we do business and how we carry on realising the vision of CKL. However, this can be quite challenging in Nigeria, especially because there is a need for improvement in implementing processes, structure and enforcement of laws.

Based on a 2016 report released by the World Economic Forum, it was highlighted that the construction sector ranks among the most prone to corruption across global industries. This can be attributed largely to the distinctive nature of this field. Notably, contracts and undertakings within this sector tend to be sizable and exclusive in nature. These intricacies contribute to challenges in effectively monitoring construction projects, thereby creating opportunities for unethical practices like bribery and embezzlement to flourish. Moreover, the majority of construction endeavours involve a multitude of stakeholders, including governmental bodies, clients, contractors, subcontractors, consultants and suppliers, among others. The industry worldwide is also known to have relatively low profit margins (3-5%).

In Nigeria, this is applicable to contractors who carry out

their business with integrity. However, the notion in the country is that profit margins exceed 40%; this is definitely not so. At times, companies that do not act with integrity collude with stakeholders to inflate contract sums and create phony claims for fluctuations and variations. In the process, innocent clients are made to overpay for projects or taxpayers' contributions are used to cover inflated costs for projects and services. When this happens, we citizens are all losers.

In my experience doing business ethically, you will win some and lose some; however, integrity pays in ways you least expect! I remember over a one-week period, I received two phone calls from two different officials of two big companies (one of them a Fortune-500 company with operations worldwide), asking that we accept to pay bribes in exchange for help with the award of the projects, which were totally unrelated. In line with our corporate values, we declined to pay, and we lost both projects. In May 2017, while on a flight from Johannesburg to Lagos, I had a conversation with a woman who worked in the same office as my sister. She was on a committee that had awarded a project to a company to construct a cooperative society facility. When we arrived in Lagos, I offered this woman a ride home, but I needed a permit for some regulated items I was carrying. Another passenger with the same items got through after paying a $15 bribe. I decided not to and left the items behind. I dropped off the woman and went home. Three days later, I received a call from her office, and our discussions led to the re-award of the project, this time to my own company. Remarkably, within just six weeks, we secured one of the most significant projects in our company's history up to that point. During the talks preceding the award, her boss inquired whether I was a pastor, to which I responded in the negative. Little did we know, the company was facing integrity problems with the existing contractor on the site and was actively seeking a more trustworthy replacement. My honesty at the airport led to our company being chosen for a project. I refused to offer a bribe, and it showed the decision-makers the integrity they were looking for. At CKL, we have continued to work ethically for over thirty years, resulting in repeat business with certain companies over the years.

CONCLUSION

Being a leader means having a compelling vision, being able to convince others, caring about people and always doing the right thing even when no-one is watching. Construction Kaiser Limited grew from a thought to a thriving company through a blend of vision, persuasion and empathy.

ABOUT IGBUAN OKAISABOR

Igbuan Okaisabor, an accomplished civil engineer, is the founder and CEO of Construction Kaiser Limited (CKL), a Nigerian construction firm with a three-decade legacy and an impressive portfolio spanning industrial, residential and commercial projects across diverse regions in Nigeria.

Dedicated to enforcing industry standards, Igbuan serves on numerous boards and organisations, holding key roles such as president of the Nigerian-German Chamber of Commerce and council member of FOCI. He also channels his efforts into initiatives like the Lagos State Employability Support Project.

As a fellow of NICE and a Harvard Business School alumnus,

Igbuan extends his impact through the Kaiser Foundation for Social Development, focusing on empowering and developing youths. He advocates for creating shared value (CSV) to address societal needs through innovative business models.

When I have this, I'll do this … *If that is your line of thinking, even if you get what you think you need to optimise, maximise or construct what you desire, you won't be able to. Because fundamentally, if you can't do that with what you have right now, why would you be granted more? Think of it this way – if you're a CEO of an organisation that has mismanaged all resources, will you be given more? No, you'd be fired. So, the same ethos applies to yourself. If you can't see what is available to you now, you won't be given more. This is a cornerstone of entrepreneurial thinking, and a local powerhouse in the Australian construction industry is the next co-author, who will show you exactly how it's done …*

2

RESOURCEFULNESS AS A LIFE-CHANGING ABILITY

BY MEL GHOLAMI

WHAT IS ONE THING YOU WOULD TELL A PERSON?

Within each of us lies an innate skill that, when nurtured, becomes a life-changing ability: resourcefulness.

WHY?

Whether you're at the start of your career or your journey is already well underway, being the most resourceful person you can be is the wisest advice I can offer you. And being one of only 12% of women in construction nationwide, a young woman in an executive role, a partner, a mother, businesswoman and from a non-English speaking background, I've learnt a thing or two about resourcefulness!

Resourcefulness, at its core, is inextricably linked to survival. We instinctively find ways to adapt, seek out people and communities to share a mutual support with, use creative ways to problem-solve and continuously evolve our approach. But when resourcefulness is harnessed, honed and used purposefully throughout your personal and professional life, it's transformed into an invaluably powerful trait. It will see you through every challenge, obstacle and opportunity that comes your way in the industry – and in life.

So, what do I mean by 'resourcefulness'?

Becoming a highly resourceful person means possessing the ability to make the most of what you have. It means tapping into your creativity to find solutions, workarounds and innovative pathways forward. It means genuine relationship building through networking, creating positive workplace cultures and surrounding yourself with the right people who will almost invariably become a crucial resource to you. It empowers you to confidently navigate challenges, adapt to new situations and seize opportunities to learn and grow.

Resourcefulness is being proactive in seeking out connections, information and knowledge you can bank and draw on when you need it. It's utilising your resources wisely and efficiently, and the ability to look strategically at what you have in front of you and make it work.

Here are some of the ways being resourceful has lifted me to where I am today:

STARTING PLANIX

My resourcefulness and the industry connections throughout my early career meant that I had developed a reputation in the project management space. I was approached to deliver project management for hospitals, and this was the opportunity to truly spread my wings that I had been waiting for my whole life.

But it takes a whole lot of resources to launch a company, and I had to dig deep.

In the early days of Planix, resourcefulness was an absolute necessity. I wore every hat imaginable. I was the CEO, CFO, COO, HR director, IT director, marketing director – and all on a budget. I persevered through finding all the resources I needed to perform all these roles, until I was able recruit my amazing team of people to wear all those hats for me.

PROBLEM-SOLVING

Some of the best innovative solutions come from the biggest problems, and as the old proverb goes, 'Necessity is the mother of invention.' Being resourceful gives you the power to explore a problem from every angle and use your creativity to discover an inventive solution.

EFFICIENCY

Lack of efficiency is a pain point for every company, team and professional. It costs time, money (sometimes, your sanity) and valuable resources better spent on growth. Resourcefulness finds a better way. It cuts through the cycle of frustration and indecision by allowing you to identify the most effective strategies and make the best use of the tools and networks at your disposal.

ADAPTABILITY

Life is filled with unexpected twists, turns and changes we're seldom ready for. Being resourceful empowers you to better adapt to change, pivot your direction when you need to and build your resilience in the face of adversity.

GROWTH AND LEARNING

From beginning to end, your personal and professional life are an ongoing growth journey. You grow by learning, and you learn by seeking out knowledge from others. Resourcefulness encourages a growth mindset by allowing yourself to be open to learning from others, be relentless in your pursuit of knowledge and constantly looking at the different perspectives of others to expand your own resources.

SELF-RELIANCE

You are the driver of your own success, and resourcefulness is the fuel you'll use to race forward to achieve your goals. When you're resourceful, you stop waiting for the answers to come to you (because they rarely do). Instead, you dig deep into your toolbelt for solutions and become more self-reliant, confident and empowered to take control of your life and every decision you make.

I have discussed the ways in which resourcefulness is an essential life ability in every setting.

So, by now you are probably wondering, *How do I become more resourceful?* Simply answered, it takes time, patience and practise. It's hard work, but what in this life *isn't?*

As I said in the beginning of the chapter, resourcefulness in its purest foundational form is linked to survival. But *mastering* your resourcefulness is linked to success.

The three attributes I devotedly live by and owe much of my success to are what I like to call 'the 3Ps'. Passion, persistence and people. The 3Ps embody resourcefulness, and I channel it into the actions I take every day. Let's break them down.

PASSION

Whatever I do, I *must* find passion in and be passionate about, because that's how you become the best at what you do. Passionate people attract passionate people, and before long, you've surrounded yourself with like-minded and driven individuals. Passion pushes your resourcefulness to discover more, strive for more and achieve more.

PERSISTENCE

When you love something, you never give up on it. It's simply not an option. Whether it's chasing a dream, grinding away at a project or helping yourself or others to grow, you dig into your resourcefulness, be persistent and never give up on yourself or others.

PEOPLE

People skills aren't something you're born with. Learning different communication styles, strategies and preferences of a diverse range of people sounds like a lifetime of learning. But I can't stress enough how important people and your connections and relationships with them are to your personal and professional growth. This relates to your clients, stakeholders and, most importantly, your staff. Investing in your relationships builds a level of mutual trust, respect and connection that serves as the foundations for the success you build along your career journey.

People are an irrefutably critical part of your resourcefulness. The networks you build from the very beginning all the way through your career will serve as an endless resource of information, advice, guidance and support that you can call on.

An example that's firmly cemented in my mind and that I reflect on frequently happened very early in my career. It was one of my first jobs and I hadn't had the time or opportunity to start building my industry networks and connections. I was still at university and started work in a whole new world filled with industry-specific terminology, processes and procedures I'd yet to have a chance to master in a hands-on environment. I was working onsite when the site manager approached me and asked me to build an 'EOT register' for him, and then – in the true fast-paced nature of construction – out the door he went. There were no instructions, there was no guidance and here I was tasked with something I'd never even heard of before. I wracked my brain for what an EOT register could be, and these were the days where Google was still in its infancy and the information I needed wasn't available with a simple search and click. But there was a task that needed to be done, and I wasn't about to let a few small obstacles get in the way of my success. So, I dug deep into some of the only resources I had at my disposal at that point – people. I started making calls to my university friends and asked, 'What on *earth* is an EOT register?!' After a few phone calls (and a few nervous laughs), I discovered what an 'extension of time register' was. Once I knew, I got straight to work on building a comprehensive and detailed EOT register that would become a key resource for the company.

It was from that moment I realised the critical importance of resourcefulness not simply as a personality trait, but as the people and networks I would connect myself with personally and professionally throughout my successful career. When you nurture your people and connections, you become part of a community that can guide you with their knowledge, and that you can help in guiding with your own.

When I look at all my successes, learning curves (steep ones) and how resourcefulness has played a part in each and every step, it cements my belief in it being an unequivocally critical ability worthy of your time and devotion.

Like all things in life, resourcefulness takes work.

It takes a willingness to grow, patience to look for solutions calmly, creatively and strategically, resilience to withstand setbacks, a thirst for knowledge and a passion for learning.

And most importantly, it takes people.

Everything and everyone that will go into developing your resourcefulness is at your fingertips, and I can promise you, it will pay off as you move through your career and your life.

ABOUT MEL GHOLAMI

Mel Gholami is a passionate entrepreneur and the managing director and founder of Planix Projects, a specialist multi-award-winning project management company where she has delivered over $5 billion of property and infrastructure projects within Australia. A pioneer of the construction industry as one of the first women to have founded a project management firm in 2012, Mel uses her successful company *as a platform for the advocacy and mentorship of women in business.*

With a Bachelor of Engineering (Civil) and a Diploma in Engineering Practice, Mel's accomplished and continuous success in the construction industry has helped set the pace for young women nationwide looking to enter the industry and kickstart their careers. As the winner of the Australian Business Champion Icon award, Mel's contribution to the construction industry is widely recognised and she takes every opportunity to share her hard-earned wisdom gathered throughout her entrepreneurial journey.

Mel's philanthropic work and women's advocacy sit firmly beside her love for business and the construction industry, where she uses her profile and resources to raise charitable funds and inspire women to chase their dreams.

Have you ever walked through squares, plazas, historic grounds? Do you get a sense of awe, precision, harmony, as you marvel at the perfection of every line? How your body moves seamlessly, even intuitively in these spaces? Or even modern spaces, which are so melodic, so prime for a significant human experience that you can't even put into words why this space was so moving. There's a reason for this, and Fabio Grilli shares the driving principles, honed by masters of space and feeling over time …

3

Designing Meaningful Spaces: The Power of Individual Experience

BY FABIO GRILLI

What is one thing you would tell a person?

Prioritise individual experiences in architecture, considering them as the driving force to create meaningful and emotive spaces.

Why?

To you, approaching the world of architecture and construction with an uncontainable thirst for knowledge and passion, I want to share some lessons I've learned on my journey – lessons that have shaped my approach to practising this profession and understanding the mission to which we are called.

In the dynamic universe of design and architecture, the apprenticeship is the fertile ground where the roots of your creative career are sown. Tackle this path with curious eyes and hands ready to shape ideas into tangible projects. It's not just a mandatory passage but a growth laboratory where every experience, even the most modest, contributes to building your skill set. Beyond captivating presentations and design magazines, the real magic lies in the details of the process. Embrace every opportunity to work in the field, from marginal involvements in projects to more complex challenges. Each step will contribute to defining your style and shaping your approach to design.

Patience becomes your travel companion as you refine your skills. Every drawing, every revision and every project are crucial steps in your evolution. Don't fear obstacles but embrace them as growth opportunities. Your dedication to the process, coupled with an insatiable thirst for learning, is the key to navigating through challenges and emerging as a design professional. Creativity flourishes when given space for experimentation. Don't be afraid to explore new ideas, challenge the status quo and leave your unique mark. Find the balance between aesthetics and functionality, as effective design goes beyond visual appearance, embracing user experience and the surrounding context.

In the search for your space, don't underestimate the importance of learning from those already on the path to success. Working well in a team is an essential skill in our field. Collect mentorships like precious gems. Work side by side with professionals you admire, immerse yourself in their experiences and be inspired by their passion. This will not only shorten your learning curve but also introduce you to a network of connections that will prove invaluable on your journey. Jim Rohn wrote that we are the 'average of the five people we spend the most time with'.

If we apply this concept to architecture, it can be said that our identity as designers depends mainly on the personalities we will be around in the early years of work: choose the professional studios where you can learn the trade well, even if it involves economic sacrifices and stress, but this will be more than compensated when you are free to take flight independently. Below, I want to summarise the cardinal principles I've learned along the way, hoping they will be inspiring to you.

The most common representation of architecture often tends to emphasise the aesthetic factors that characterise design, reducing the complex design process to a mere production of beautiful three-dimensional figures to be consumed quickly in some magazine or captured in an Instagram story. There is absolutely nothing wrong with being captivated by the aesthetic impact a beautiful building can generate, as long as this factor doesn't become the sole objective of the designer, namely creating a photogenic object, made of appearance without substance, ignoring the fundamental element for which a building has a reason to exist: improving the life of those who use it.

Imagine entering a space – be it your bedroom, an office, a public building, a square or a park. What you must understand is that this space is not simply a physical place; it is a context that will shape the experiences of people, including your own, becoming the stage for countless life stories. Every project you undertake must always have the user's perspective as the generative principle.

One of the first concepts I learned is, therefore, the importance of individual experience. Every person carries a unique set of experiences that translate into needs and preferences. So, when you design, don't just think about forms and structures in themselves, but consider above all the people who will inhabit or use that place. Making each space unique, adapting it to individual stories, is the key to creating places that are more than simple buildings; they become refuges, spaces of inspiration and comfort. To achieve this, not only do you need to set aside your preconceived design ideas and adopt an open and multisensory approach, but there is something more. Ask people what they want from the spaces they will inhabit, don't be attracted only to the needs that will overwhelm them. This is one of the thoughts that emerged from collaboration with the psychiatrist/psychotherapist Filippo Ruggeri, whose thinking – while recognising its importance – distances itself from a paradigm almost entirely devoted to the care of needs to bring desire back to the centre of space (vital and architectural); as highlighted by him, it is essential that the unconscious dimension of the individual and society is not stifled by an enticing logic of consumption and needs but is listened to and welcomed to generate a creative space, and therefore alive, of speech, thought and work.

The key to expanding this horizon of knowledge is the exploration and understanding of ways of life different from yours. Despite today having immediate access to 'street views' worldwide through a simple smartphone, the true cognitive exploration of reality can be considered full and effective only if perceived through the five senses we have – that is, only through physical travel. The most effective way to understand different cultures is to savour their most everyday aspects, made up of real practices, the subjective tensions of individuals born and raised in cultural contexts very different from ours. Stepping out of your comfort zone and putting your habits and certainties at stake is an exercise that can be tiring but ultimately improves our ability to face challenges and better understand the world around us. Curiosity and understanding of what is different are the foundation of cultural growth, the foundation of the architect's profession.

Be aware of the power of spaces to evoke emotions. Architecture is an emotional language in itself. Every line, every material, every detail contributes to shaping the emotions of those who enter. You must try to understand how every design choice can influence people's emotional state. For example, natural light and certain colour scales can create an atmosphere of calm and vitality. Your task is to do it intentionally, to communicate positive emotions. You will understand that design is not just a matter of appearance but of sensations. A bright and airy environment can convey a sense of spaciousness and optimism, a place with warm colours and natural materials can evoke a welcoming and familiar atmosphere, while a minimal and monochromatic space can facilitate internal reflection.

Sometimes, it is better to minimise architectural intervention to fully enjoy the surrounding context: there is no better setting than a scene to observe, whether it's a sky or a sea, a skyline or an avenue. Don't focus solely on the material of the construction itself, leverage what the surrounding environment has to offer to our senses.

Architecture is a bridge between art and science, an art that shapes the daily life of people, that is, the cultural expression of an entire society. I invite you to investigate within yourself and understand what drives your desire to embark on this path. You will see that at the beginning of your journey, you will face difficulties in finding space to express your ideas, but I advise you not to focus on the obstacles but to leverage your desire to create something beautiful for others, as this will represent the true measure of your success.

ABOUT FABIO GRILLI

As the head of design and development at Emaar Properties, Fabio brings extensive experience in both the design and real estate industries. He has played a pivotal role in the development of large-scale masterplans, including Dubai Creek Harbour, Emaar Beachfront and Dubai Hills Estate, among others.

His contributions extend to ongoing projects across the MENA region and Europe.

Fabio is a sought-after speaker in the industry, sharing insights on sustainable design, mixed-use development and vertical cities at worldwide events and prestigious universities.

Holding a Master's Degree in Architecture and Urban Planning from the University of Ferrara, he has worked with international firms in the Netherlands, Italy and the UAE.

Do you operate from a baseline of urgency? Not out of a place of constantly running out, but from the point that there's just so much to experience, to achieve, to create, to be, to do? This creates an individual who has an immense zest for life and is extremely uplifting for their positive disposition. Ronda Conger is that individual, an industry titan who only leaves you with a fire in your heart and a feeling that you have a personal team vouching for you to go bigger, and of course … faster. Strap yourself in, you're about to experience a wild ride.

4

GO FASTER

BY RONDA CONGER

WHAT IS ONE THING YOU WOULD TELL A PERSON?
Go faster.

WHY?
I have been in love with new home construction for the last thirty years. As I look back, my advice is simple.

Go faster.

Your ability to say yes is in direct proportion to how fast you will go in this career. But I had to say a very important no before I said yes to this life-changing career of thirty years in construction.

It was 1993, I was newly engaged and living in Las Vegas, Nevada, with my fiancé. We were fresh out of college, and my fiancé had taken a job with Bechtel Construction. Once we hit Vegas, I decided I needed a job, so I called a temp agency. They put me to work that afternoon at a company in the cellular tower sales and marketing industry. I loved it. It was fast-paced, I was consistently asked to take on more, do more, learn more, and the place was bumping. PERFECT. I stayed late, I worked hard and became the go-to person.

I'll never forget the first time I saw the most impressive businesswoman pull up outside of our building and park in the front in her baby-blue Jaguar. She got out, dressed to the nines and ready to throw down. I quickly leaned over to my colleague and said, 'Who is that? I must know!' I was quickly told that she was Michelle – a high-up executive from corporate out of California – and to not make eye contact with her. Still laughing today about that suggestion. As months rolled by, I would see her from time to time, and on one particular occasion when I had stayed late to finish up, my whole life would change in an instant.

She stopped by my desk on the way out. She said, 'Are you Ronda?' *Ummm, yes, yes, I am! WHAT?!?* is all my twenty-two-year-old brain kept shouting at me. *WHY IS SHE TALKING TO ME?* She then proceeded to tell me that she had heard about me, my work ethic, yes being my favourite word, loved my hunger for more knowledge and wanted to know if I wanted to be her assistant to help her start up and run her own division in Las Vegas.

Any guesses on what my answer was? YES. The answer was a resounding yes. Quite honestly, it was a very passionate fuck yes.

Consider this a brief intermission in our story. This is important.

GO FASTER LESSON #1:

Don't wait to be told what to do. Go do it.

Don't wait to be trained or given all the information. Read, watch, find and seek it out.

Your work hours and key areas given to you by your employer are the bare minimum they expect out of you. Do more. Seriously, do more.

There is no set time line or path. You decide how fast you move up based on your attitude, actions and energy.

Be so good they can't ignore you.

Where was I?

Oh yes, baby-blue Jaguar, new management role, new division to start up and run alongside one hell of a mentor. She threw me in the deep end and said figure it out.

We pulled up to our new office space and here were her directions:

- You need one HR person, two salespeople, two compliance and one receptionist hired by the end of the week. *(It was Tuesday.)*
- They will all need desks, chairs, phones, computers, paper, files, paper clips and file cabinets by then as well.
- Monday of next week, I expect to return to a fully functioning office.

She threw the office keys at me, said good luck and walked out the front door. She left me standing there with my mouth wide open, which I then turned to a very big smile. I love a challenge.

I worked from sun-up to sundown for the next six days. We were up and running Monday morning 8am sharp.

Small, friendly reminder, this story takes place in Las Vegas,

Nevada, aka Sin City. This is an important piece to the story.

We were one hell of a team. I managed all aspects of the office and team, and she flew in once a week or so. There were several appreciation bonuses given in lovely white envelopes with large bills. Life was good. We were approximately nine months in, and I could not have been happier.

The day I'm about to describe will forever be ingrained in my heart and head. A snapshot in time that is frozen, a polaroid picture you hang on your mirror so you never forget, an event that seems surreal.

This isn't life? Right?

Michelle calls me Wednesday morning and says she will be in the office at 10am to meet with me. Standard practice. This time, she blows in, shuts the door behind us, sits across the desk with a very large white envelope. My first thought is … *She is loving our team, my results, our division's success.*

I WAS DEAD WRONG.

She proceeded to thank me for everything I have done for her and this division. She slid the very large envelope across the table.

Her instructions were as follows:

- We will be raided by the FBI at approximately 4:59pm today.
- You need to immediately lay off all employees and have them leave the building with severance. Which can be found in the envelope.
- You have seven hours to shred all corporate files and leave the building.
- You are no longer employed with the company. Thank you for your service.

She slid my envelope across the table and thanked me. She told me I would go far in this life. Once again, she walked out of that building, turned around and said, 'Good luck, kid.' She drove off in her baby-blue Jaguar. I have never seen or heard from her since.

GO FASTER LESSON #2

Say yes.

   Don't be afraid to do hard things, new things.
   Accept the challenge.
   Opportunities come in all shapes and sizes. Be flexible.

Here I was, unemployed, planning a wedding, and I decided that I needed a break. *I should lay by the pool, work on my tan and work on the wedding,* I thought.

I have this amazing stepmother that has two rules in life … you are either working or you are learning. It does not include tanning or a pool. She lovingly told me I could go find another job OR I could go get my real estate license so I could buy my husband a new house for our wedding. I begrudgingly said yes.

I had zero plans of doing real estate. ZERO. Not on my vision board, not in my goals, not on my life plan. I would buy us a house, end of story. As I was going through real estate school, I had this amazing instructor who was a retired NFL quarterback named Teddy. He kept telling me I needed to meet a friend of his that worked for KB Homes. That I would love her and new home construction. I said no (weird, I know), but I did.

I said no thanks. I'm not interested in a career in real estate.

One night after a full day of real estate class, I'm sitting on my sofa watching TV with my fiancé and the news comes on. The news anchor is in front of the Hard Rock, and his story is about the two open positions at the Hard Rock Cafe that only come available every couple of years. The waitress position roughly makes six figures and has a very competitive hiring gauntlet. The news anchor tells me that day one of the job fair starts tomorrow at 1pm and please bring your résumé.

I flew off the sofa and said, 'I'm doing it!!'

My fiancé said, 'Of course you are.'

I got my résumé, I got all gussied up, and I headed down to Hard Rock Cafe. Well, unbeknownst to me there would be close to five hundred people in line. The line was outside the building, around the building and into the parking lot. There were news crews everywhere. It was insane.

I got in line and waited for hours and hours to get to the front door, just to have an opportunity. I'll never forget what happened next. I was standing in line and there was this girl next to me. We're talking and she asks me, 'What's in your hand?'

She didn't have a piece of paper in her hand. I did. I replied with, 'Well, this is my résumé.' And she replies with, 'Why'd you bring your résumé? They don't need it.' And I was like, 'Well, the newscaster yesterday said to bring it.' To which she replied, 'I think it's no big deal. This is a waitress job, who cares?'

Hard Rock Cafe cares. That's who. We got up to the front door and the person was gatekeeping, not even letting you in the door. All they were doing was looking at you, greeting you and taking your résumé. And I noticed as I got closer and closer to the line, the people who didn't have a résumé were sent off to the right of the building. And the people who had a résumé, they took it from you and handed you a card with your next interview time and then said the following:

See you tomorrow. Be ready for anything.

What? Just be ready for anything? I'm ready.

GO FASTER LESSON #3
Be ready for anything.

Did I get the job?!?!

As Paul Harvey, the famous radio talk show host, would say … *Now for the rest of the story.* While I was waiting to hear back from Hard Rock Cafe on whether or not I made the cut, I received a phone call from Liesel Williams from KB Homes, the fifth-largest builder in the nation. She said that Teddy, my real estate instructor, said we had to meet. Could I swing by her office tomorrow around 9am? Yes, yes, I could. We spent three hours together that Thursday morning, her telling me all the reasons I am going to love new home construction. She spoke of growth, opportunity, knowledge, making an impact, financial rewards and endless potential. And I spent the morning telling her it wasn't part of my plan. I must admit, we hit it off. I loved hearing her stories and about her success in the industry. I thanked her for the coffee and wished her well. She said, 'See you in the morning. Sales meeting starts at 9am in the main office.'

That night at dinner, my fiancé and I laughed about the crazy turn of events over the last couple of weeks. I was sitting on that same sofa after dinner when my phone rang. It was the Hard Rock Cafe.

I got the job. Did you hear me? I GOT THE JOB.

The next day at 9am I reported to KB Homes for my very first sales meeting. I lovingly thanked Hard Rock Cafe for teaching me so much. For the job, for the opportunity. It's been thirty years since that first Friday morning in new home construction.

I was all-in for my new career. My new path. I couldn't learn fast enough. I said yes to every department and position that needed filled. In my first four years at KB Homes, I worked in the following departments: sales, design studio, warranty, finance and marketing. We moved out of state, and I went to work for a local land developer and homebuilder. They had zero openings for me. I said pay me nothing, let me be an intern, it doesn't matter. This is my passion. I wasn't going to wait for the perfect job opening, the perfect conditions, the perfect pay. They brought me on as an assistant, then salesperson, then warranty, then marketing, then director of sales and marketing.

GO FASTER LESSON #4

Stop waiting for the right conditions, the perfect opportunities.
Luck has to catch you working.

I worked with that company for another six years. I soaked up as much as I could from the owner and his son. I read book after book on all things construction. I went to conference after conference. My goal was to be the absolute best at what I do. I invested in myself. I didn't wish or hope that someone would train me, show me, pay for my books and conferences. I am utterly shook that I have found that most people stop learning once they get out of school or once they land a job.

They believe they are done.

I completely disagree.

Do you want more?

Do you want growth?

Do you want opportunities?

Do you want more money?

Do you want a better title?

Do you want a career you love?

Do you want a life you're proud of?

If you want all of the items above, then you need to *go faster.*

For the past twenty years, I have been insanely proud of being the vice president of CBH Homes. I knew very early on that this is what I wanted. This has been one hell of a journey. I have zero regrets. The Hard Rock Cafe was tempting, but this is my life, this is my passion.

Stop waiting and start doing (to go faster).

Say yes (to go faster).

Do more. No really, do more (to go faster).

Try and try again (to go faster).

Learn, dive in headfirst, and just soak it all up (to go faster).

Be fearless (to go faster).

Go faster.

ABOUT RONDA CONGER

Some say she was raised by wolves, others claim truckers. No matter her upbringing, this superwoman has flourished in a male-dominated industry for thirty years. As vice president of CBH Homes, Idaho's largest homebuilder, Ronda leads the CBH troops daily and has overseen all areas of the company for the past twenty years.

Ronda firmly believes that winning is a habit. She's been named the 2021 NAHB Woman of the Year by the National Association of

Home Builders, and recently recognised by Women We Admire as a Top 50 Women Leaders of the Mountain Region.

Serving others is important to Ronda. As a businesswoman, professional speaker and author, Ronda is on a mission to spread a movement with her five books: Better Human, Better Thinking, You Go First, Leading Through Extraordinary Times *and her latest book* New Market. New You.

It's been rumoured her high energy and passion come from shotgunning Red Bulls daily, but she'll tell you it comes from her incredibly hot husband, Jim Conger (just ask her), and her two sons.

She thanks the heavens each day for this incredible journey and is so very grateful for the opportunity to serve and love all those that she comes in contact with.

Laurice Temple was the first person I met in the construction industry, back in 2013, and I recall the interactions fondly as a person of great fortitude, knowing and depth. As our journeys respectively unfolded and chance interactions occurred over the years, Laurice too kept going from strength to strength. She remains one of the most long-standing industry leaders I know, who still has that love and fight in her to transform the industry from the root cause, and it was a pleasure to discover her secret to it all ...

5

BUILDING A CURIOSITY MINDSET

BY LAURICE TEMPLE

WHAT IS ONE THING YOU WOULD TELL A PERSON?
Be OVERTLY curious!

WHY?
I have absolutely loved my thirty-plus-year career in construction. In this industry, never are two days the same; whether it be the different people you get to engage with, the supply chain challenges, the changes in weather or just the circumstances of the day, all of which led to having to rethink innovative solutions to the challenges presented.

From this perspective, the most important thing that has made a difference in my career is to be open, non-judgemental and inquisitive, i.e. be curious – which allows us as humans to be able to create new ideas and innovate, particularly when faced with unexpected problems.

Curiosity in plain terms is 'the desire to know'. But what I mean by being curious is to expand on and go deeper than that and include the desire to know MORE and to take the opportunity to look at things differently to 'what I THINK I know'.

I must admit, getting curious has taken a lot of courage and intention, in my experience, as it is so easy to get stuck in the rut of being bound to our own biases, thoughts and past experiences. Curiosity allows us to go beyond what we already think we know. It prevents us from being arrogant, judgemental and stagnating.

'Expertise is what you know. Humility is knowing what you don't know. Curiosity is how much you want to learn.'
– Adam Grant

Not surprisingly, Albert Einstein was known for encouraging curiosity: 'I am neither especially clever nor especially gifted. I am only very, very curious.' Einstein didn't see himself as overly talented, but he was firmly set in the idea that imagination was more powerful and important than knowledge, and that curiosity was the foundation of imagination. We certainly know how much his curiosity has changed the world in which we live today!

The construction industry is a wonderfully rewarding, albeit an intense and stressful, industry. We build things that touch every part of human lives which is incredibly inspiring and amazing! But as the world evolves around us, we need to adapt, change and be future-focused to be able to meet the new needs. Which drives the critical importance to stay curious to what those new needs are to be able to innovate and build accordingly.

I've found that it's easy to fall prey to the mindset of 'this is the way we do things' (arrogance) which keeps us stuck in the past ways of working (stagnation). I am grateful that a curiosity mindset seed was planted early on in my career. The first one I remember is when I was provided a chance to chat with a very seasoned construction manager who emphatically impressed upon me to not accept what everyone else said but to question and be invested in the solutions myself. He then went on to share a story, by way of example, about how he came up with a unique way to build a large airplane hangar by resequencing the works and building the roof first before putting the walls up. This thinking was primarily driven by taking into consideration the severe weather patterns during the year and to figure out the most effective and efficient way to build. He was chastised for such a 'silly idea' as they had never built one like that before; however, the team worked through his innovative design and ended up building it that way. This in turn saved the project millions of dollars and completed the project six months ahead of schedule. That story has always stuck with me and has helped give me courage when facing backlash on my curious thinking.

I don't deny – to get curious can take courage as it's that fear of reprisal for asking silly questions. So, when I went on my first onsite project assignment where we were building an anechoic chamber for the US Navy, it took a great amount of courage for me to ask the superintendent, Jerry, if he would be open to come and get me whenever we were starting a new activity and have him walk me through it. He looked at me sideways, sort of grunted at me and after what seemed like eternity, nodded yes. It became a delight for me when he would open the trailer door and scream my name, and in turn I would grab my hard hat and go running out (you never hold up a superintendent!). He would graciously, in his very gruff manner, take me through the works and make sure I understood the activity, materials, resourcing, safety, cost and productivity. He encouraged me to be curious and ask lots of questions, and to 'never accept what the site engineers told me' (always then our inside joke which created greater respect and trust as he knew I was going to challenge). It was yet another great springboard into my curious mindset for my career!

I've come to realise that there are a lot of very clever people in the industry who have a plethora of knowledge and experience. But I've also realised that no-one is 'all-knowing' or can see into the future. Whether it be the impacts of climate change, evolving technologies, new products and services, more effective ways of working including creating psychologically safe places to work are all challenges that we are currently dealing with on top of the daily changes that occur. Consequently, we need everyone in the industry to bring their own life experiences, knowledge and their curiosity to help tackle the challenges with diverse thought and insight.

To provide further perspective in why it's important to get curious, it is estimated that in 2023 we are generating 328.77 million terabytes of data EACH DAY! This not only means there is new data being created, but it also highlights the importance of ensuring we challenge a culture of 'this is the way we do it around here'. That kind of mindset won't allow people to innovate and utilise new data.

One of the key complexities around being curious and challenging the status quo, however, is that, as research shows, to challenge can easily lead to others being defensive. As stated in a December 2020 *Science News* article, 'Humans have a primary psychological need to be valued and included by others, to feel that they are good and appropriate group members or relationship partners.' It went on further to say, 'This research shows that defensiveness is strengthened by negative social responses but is reduced when people feel secure in their group identity, respected and valued.'[1]

> *'Defensive behaviours are common responses when people feel personally attacked but can undermine our ability to identify problems and find solutions.'*
> *– Professor Michael Wenzel et al*

So, how do we challenge each other and yet ensure people also feel respected and valued? This makes it imperative to not only intentionally create a culture of inviting in curiosity and challenge dissenting voices, but also address defensive behaviour to ensure people feel respected. In my own experiences, I relied heavily on my courage, confidence and outgoing personality as a foundation in being curious. However, I still had to deal with defensive behaviour from others who didn't like being challenged. This highlights the importance for organisations to create a culture that allows all this to happen. Research shows that in order to be curious and share with others, we need to create an environment that makes it psychologically safe to do so. Psychological safety is defined as 'the belief that you won't be punished or humiliated for speaking up with ideas, questions,

---

1 sciencedaily.com/releases/2020/12/201201103610.htm#:~:text=%22Humans%20have%20a%20 primary%20psychological,threatened%2C%20driving%20a%20defensive%20response

concerns or mistakes'. It is about feeling safe to take interpersonal risks, to speak up, to disagree openly, to surface concerns without fear of negative repercussions. Research on this topic shows when people don't feel psychologically safe, we stay silent or shut down.

To help organisations create such cultures, the new ISO 45003 'OHS management – psychological health and safety at work: guidelines for managing psychosocial risks' was developed. It is helping create a new emphasis and understanding on the basic compliance framework to help create psychologically safe spaces, through identifying psychosocial hazards. It is imperative to create safe spaces to allow people to speak up, innovate and create differently.

Greater still, when building greater psychologically safe spaces, it helps build trust within the team to speak up and to feel heard. This in turn creates greater-performing teams and increases productivity.

In summary, challenging my own thinking and building a curious mindset has helped me be more innovative to solve complex and challenging problems. But being curious can be challenging and feel confronting to others, so creating psychologically safe spaces helps everyone feel respected and valued. This in turn creates higher-performing teams. Higher-performing teams generate greater profitability. Win-win! Curiosity is definitely a game changer!

ABOUT LAURICE TEMPLE
Laurice is a business consultant with the bulk of her project career experience in project management of large infrastructure projects in the United States, Hong Kong, Singapore, Thailand and Australia.

She is also a non-executive board director on several boards.

Laurice is the founder of Ripple Affect Institute which specialises in business improvement via coaching, mentoring and strategic leadership initiatives. She is a known proponent of co-creating positive impact by assisting clients in integrating innovation, continuous improvement and wellbeing mindsets in their organisations in order to achieve greater success.

Laurice has a Bachelor of Science in Construction Management, is accredited through Australian Institute of Project Management as a Certified Practicing Portfolio Executive (CPPE), has a Certificate IV in Frontline Project Management, and a graduate of the Australian Institute Company Directors course (GAICD), a licensee of Michelle McQuaid's Wellbeing Lab, and Gateway Reviewer.

If you look at the industry as a whole, you cannot confidently say it values wealth, freedom, truth, real integrity. Half of the values plastered on walls can come down, because the poster and the behaviour do not match. Living by values also doesn't come with terms and conditions. I.e. 'I value honesty but only when others are honest to me, and I don't have to be.' It would be a book unto itself about the contradictions of the industry. But then you have exemplary leaders like Gianluca Pascale, who after 'the school of hard knocks', has kept a high moral disposition to upholding values. What are values, and how do I discover them? Great question — let's find out.

6

YOUR CORE VALUES

BY GIANLUCA PASCALE

WHAT IS ONE THING YOU WOULD TELL A PERSON?
Much of your happiness resides within your core values.

WHY?
They're the fundamental starting point of the beliefs and principles that shape your character and guide your actions, decisions and behaviours. They represent the essence of who we are and what we stand for. They provide you with a clear sense of purpose, aid in decision-making, enhance your self-awareness and foster meaningful relationships. Therefore, by virtue of living and working based on your core values, you drastically reduce the amounts of struggles, aggravation and mental anguish you may otherwise encounter.

The absence of knowing, let alone not following or adhering to, your personal core values will hold you back in life. It's a sure way to attract experiences, opportunities and pretty much everything else you do not want for yourself, your career and your business. It prevents you from reaching your maximum potential and will have you on a trajectory that isn't meant for you. So, why allow that to happen?

'Values are like fingerprints. Nobody's are the same, but you leave them all over everything you do.' – Elvis Presley

The following wisdom was learned through years of experience. Some of it at extreme costs. Both financial and mental anguish. But the good news is, I got through to the other side to share these observations and lessons with you with hopes that you apply them to ensure that your journey through life is a fruitful one meant specifically for you. Because, contrary to common belief, we have a lot of say as to what comes into our life and how it unfolds.

With that said, what is your North Star? Or the hill you're willing to die on?

In other words, what is your inner compass – the part of you that knows your passion, purpose, ambition, vision and life direction you have for yourself? That something which is so important to you that you would be willing to die for it?

You may be wondering why I am leading with such heavy questions. Truth is, they're not heavy at all. The answer to these questions resides within you. They are all key factors in describing you authentically. Qualities, attributes and values that make up who you are as an individual as well as your method of operation. Core values are not something you look over your friend's shoulder and copy whatever they've listed. It takes introspection.

A deep look inside yourself to see what makes you tick.

To direct you with this, I invite you to think of your core values as guiding your behaviours, decisions and actions. Begin to identify yours by thinking about some of the best and worst moments in your life and reverse-engineer those moments to capture the core values that best describe you. Carefully dissect these moments in such a way that they identify the decisions you made or didn't make as well as deep-rooted feelings you stuck with or veered away from which produced the results that are today happy, sad, regretful or angry memories.

Remember, you are only doing this to identify, describe and subsequently adopt your personal core values, and not to relive or get stuck on the negative. There are lessons with everything in life. Some of them are obvious, and some of them take a bit more work to uncover. Either way, the beauty is that if you really pay attention and seek to learn from every moment, opportunity, decision or action, there will always be the playback available for you to review. The introspective work required to dig up your personal core values is intertwined in all of these turning points in your life.

Your foundational core values are hard-wired within you. You are born with them. There's no escaping them. Sure, some come along later in life, and some evolve as you grow wiser, but you can't outrun them. Sooner or later, if you live life to the fullest, the light switch will go off and things will start making sense. There's also the odd rude awakening that happens where you say to yourself, *Never again.* Make note of all of those. And for heaven's sake, listen to your gut. There's no better instrument we possess. It's never wrong, and it only speaks loudly once, so pay attention!

I remember a client years ago had been chasing and hounding us to work together, but something didn't feel right. I heard plenty of horror stories about how they treated their contractors and service providers and none of those were any good. But their persistence wore me down and I dropped my guard and accepted to do work with them knowing deep in my gut that our core values didn't align. True to form, on the very first project, they short-changed us on payment and gave us invalid and lame excuses as to why they didn't want to the pay full price of their contract. Not surprisingly, it had a striking resemblance to all the stories I heard of them prior. Had I stuck to my core values, I would have averted that unpleasant and avoidable experience. Fool me once, shame on me. Fool me twice, well … you know how it goes.

Once you've identified your core values, write them down. There's a process I learned a few years back that has produced explosive results for me that I'd like to share with you: wild mind writing (WMR). WMR is free associative and creative writing. You typically set a timer (I would recommend nothing less than five minutes) and mind-dump everything that comes to mind. Obviously, your intent is to write about the things that have shaped you so far. The good, the bad and the ugly and then apply what I have shared with you so far.

This also reminds me of what John Lennon and Sir Paul McCartney used to say: 'Let's write ourselves a swimming pool.' They said it out of innocence and normal working-class glee in order to actually do something and earn money. Writing your core values is no different. They will be the source of your future wealth, assuming you know and follow them.

The key is to be unwavering. Let nothing get in the way or pressure you into neglecting, bending or changing them. Worse yet, accept those of someone else. They're the framework on which we evaluate our choices. Knowing your core values will help you stay focused on things that matter to you. They will always be your litmus test and guiding light when confronted with opportunities, challenges, risks and threats. For example, they will help you decide who you let into your circle of influence, determine which company's culture you'll adapt best with along with which teammates and clients you will work best with.

Core values in construction?

Yes! Lord knows, as an industry, we lack them. I would be surprised if our industry knows what our core values are and were able to recite them. Therefore, it is imperative that you do not repeat the same mistakes the industry has made in the past. An example of which would be its lack of integrity. Rather than do what's right even when nobody's looking, our industry's preference is to do the opposite.

Many contractors and subtrades accomplish this by cutting corners. Changing materials without proper approvals. Installing less, if any, specific materials when nobody is looking. When I started in this industry, I worked in the residential industry. I remember visiting a new subdivision in a big city and personally witnessed exterior walls as well as the underside of exposed floors go covered over without any insulation, and at times even without vapour barrier. I guess the developer and subtrades' integrity went out along with the insulation and vapour barrier. What's worse, I later heard stories that building inspectors looked the other way which allowed the wrongdoers to get away with these nefarious actions.

These types of decisions are also an evident lack of pride, which in a macro sense have painted everyone with the same brush. But fear not, as there is a unique way to be a stand-out in the construction industry. Embrace your values and stand firm on what that is specifically for you.

You can also think of your core values – your highest priorities – as your built-in navigation system. Only this navigation system enables you to maintain a focused direction and provides you with clarity when:

- Determining what matters most to you.
- You align your actions with your authentic self.
- Making the right decisions for yourself.
- Prioritising what matters most to you.
- Understanding what you will and won't tolerate.

Because what we tolerate, persists. The construction industry is synonymous with Einstein's definition of insanity which is doing the same things over and over again, expecting different results. With that, we have long since tolerated many things. Most of which are not complimentary to our industry, narrative and reputation.

The irony with this is that we are responsible for building and maintaining the infrastructure that keeps communities functioning and prospering. The roads and bridges that get us to and from destinations, the homes we live in, the schools we learn in, the buildings we work in, the hospitals we heal in, the places of worship we pray in, etc.

Think about that for a moment. That's an enormous onus

that's been placed on our shoulders. Yet, as an industry overall, we're a hot mess. Most of that is self-inflicted. Some of it is due to the 'old boys' club' that's still present to this day. The type that doesn't like change and prefers status quo.

The construction industry has also aligned itself with the wrong people. We've failed to maintain a solid grasp on the overall control of our industry, thus losing it to a Faustian bargain we've made with governments, local industry associations and clients. All three being the primary sources of where we've gone for help in the past.

You might say that we've lost our North Star and clearly do not know which hill we'd be willing to die on. To acquire opportunities and riches, it costs us our core values. It costs us our identity and power. We've become a transactional industry, rather than transformational.

It's been staring at us right in the face this whole time. Core values serve as the foundation upon which all build their success.

You may say that our industry is in need of a renovation.

The truth is, we are in desperate need of individuals like yourself. People that choose this industry because they, among others, love to work with their hands, have a knack for orchestrating and coordinating things, recognise the constant learning opportunities which then parlays into skills stacking and continued growth and entrepreneurial opportunities as well as your own personal contribution to society.

Whether you choose to make a career in construction in the trades, management, or if you have your eyes set on ascending to a leadership position or even starting your own business, then your core values are not only what will get your there, they are the prerequisite to achieving.

By defining your personal identity and purpose through your core values, you are more likely to engage in activities that bring you fulfilment and contentment. This clarity can also prevent feelings of aimlessness and uncertainty, as you can confidently pursue paths that resonate with your inner beliefs and values. Your core values will help increase your performance but also contribute to a safer and more harmonious work environment.

Imagine the unfair advantage you'll have when equipped with the knowledge of what you need to live a purposeful and fulfilling life.

Remember, when it comes down to it, about all an individual has are their core values. When you sell those out, there's not much left.

ABOUT GIANLUCA PASCALE

Gianluca Pascale boasts a thirty-year career in the construction industry. As founder and head curator of the Constructors Guild, he orchestrates a transformative platform, a beacon of excellence for construction professionals. With a proven record, Gianluca guides high-level construction experts toward breakthroughs. Under his adept leadership, the Constructors Guild emerges as the epicentre of connections, impactful contributions, wisdom and collaborations, setting an unmatched industry standard.

Gianluca's dedication shines through seventeen years leading Centrecon Inc, the construction management firm he founded and led to remarkable success. As author of The Collaborative Construction Process – Build Better Together *and a distinguished speaker, he amplifies his influence. With fervent passion, Gianluca challenges construction norms, fuelled by an insatiable thirst for knowledge. He champions breaking free from stagnation, reshaping the industry's narrative and elevating its reputation.*

Sitting, thinking, sitting, thinking. Speculating, thinking, doubting, thinking. Does this sound like your typical thinking process and analysis? How many times have you been scared to get off the sidelines? I am sure you deeply considered what may have gone wrong. But had you considered what could go right? Kezya De Bragança lives in the fast lane and doesn't let the unknown bar her from movement today. How else do you think winners get the championship trophy? It's not by sitting on the sidelines – forever. It's not just any old action you take, though. What's her secret? Turn the page to discover all.

7

ADAPTIVE ACTION: KEEP THE BALL ROLLING

BY KEZYA DE BRAGANÇA

WHAT IS ONE THING YOU WOULD TELL A PERSON?

When in doubt, act. When certain, act with conviction.

WHY?

When I first set foot in the world of construction, the towering sky-scrapers, expansive townships and beautiful hotels seemed nothing short of magical. That someone could imagine a space, and in a few short years transform it to physical reality felt surreal. Over the years, as I became more deeply involved, I came to realise that the final outcomes that held me enthralled were the sum of countless small, decisive actions taken quickly every day. The magic was less in the finished outcome and more in that way thousands of micro decisions connected by actions built up to the final vision. The product of the relentless push to keep the metaphorical ball rolling.

In this business, your environment is constantly evolving and time is an invaluable asset. Every day requires a touch of creative ingenuity. I always felt like I was playing a real-life game of chess where the pieces changed unpredictably and indefinitely. I've had to think on my feet and act even faster. The recurring theme that has shaped my most formative experiences has been the indispensable power of taking action.

There is a certain poetry to taking action, a nuanced dance between thought and deed. It necessitates clarity of thought, commitment and is supremely generative. Taking action yields a trove of insights in a way only contact with reality can. The world as we know it is a product of a series of actions, iterated on over endless cycles of decisions – some intentional and some serendipitous. Never, in my experience, has the complex interplay between cause and effect been more palpable than in the construction industry.

WHY ACTION IS YOUR BEST ALLY

Action is the great unraveller, it has a unique way of dispelling uncertainty, often ushering in fresh perspectives. Action adds confidence and credibility that fuel momentum and flow. Construction projects are meant to be fluid and dynamic, evolving through a series of small actions – both right and wrong. Like a living organism, it's constantly evolving, and often in ways you can't predict.

While working on a multistorey residential project, as part of the construction team, we were armed with what we believed were perfect blueprints. We felt invincible until we broke ground and discovered an undocumented underground water line that threatened to derail everything. While some dove straight into analysis and modelling scenarios, my then-boss catalysed a rapid-response meeting with engineers, architects and utility experts. Within seventy-two hours, the water line was rerouted and construction resumed. No prizes for guessing who got the promotion. This experience was a seminal lesson for me – while planning is indispensable, the capacity to act and adapt in real time is game changing. In fact, in construction, waiting for the 'perfect' blueprint could mean never breaking ground.

Action has been my antidote to overwhelm. It breaks down mammoth tasks into manageable pieces, turns uncertainty to clarity and creates a sense of momentum that propels me forward. In fact, acting on a solid plan now usually trumps waiting for a flawless one tomorrow. Even the smallest actions can have profound effects. Showing up for that meeting on a tough day can sway the situation in your favour. Making that call to your vendor can help resolve an issue before it becomes a roadblock. Sending out that email can clear confusion and keep everyone aligned. Each action, no matter how small, brings you closer to your desired outcome. Having extolled the virtues of taking action, let's explore its nuanced form – adaptive action.

MOVING FROM ACTION TO ADAPTIVE ACTION

All of us experience that paralysing fear of getting something wrong; but wrong action is superior to no action. The consequences of your actions will steer you in the right direction. The key is to keep moving, to keep learning and to never let the fear of making a wrong decision halt your progress. Every misstep can yield valuable insights, nudge you to recalibrate and redirect your actions. Think of it as navigating a maze – hitting a dead end simply tells you which path not to take, enriching your journey with new-found knowledge.

Adaptive action transcends mere activity. It embodies the relentless pursuit of your goals and champions continuous refined action in response to new insights or changing circumstances. This iterative action, whether minor, imperfect or varied, propels you closer to the realisation of your vision. This approach negates the idea of failure because every step, whether forward or backward, contributes to the learning process, edging you closer to your desired outcome.

In embracing adaptive action, exhausting internal debates – such as, *Am I doing enough?* or, *Is this the right path?* – become redundant. The essence of this mindset is to spend more time acting and adapting, over deliberation. Each decision becomes solely about the next move, the subsequent step in the journey. Take the path of least resistance, be prepared to learn by doing and strive for progress over perfection.

This mindset cultivates a sense of unstoppable momentum; when aligned with your vision, reaching your desired outcome becomes inevitable. In this paradigm, self-doubt is replaced by an empowering sense of purpose bolstered by increasing competence.

Adaptive action cares less about perfection or elegance and more about generating momentum. It is about starting from exactly where you are, with the resources you have available to you at that moment. The approach advocates for taking rapid, small and often messy action, consistently over time. Much like progress, it isn't linear and compounds its impact over time.

ADAPTIVE MOMENTUM: A REAL-WORLD EXAMPLE OF SHILLIM ESTATE

In spearheading the development of a 3,500 acre private estate situated within a UNESCO World Heritage site, our journey was one that transcended the conventional constructs of architecture and construction. From infrastructural development to the extraordinary cultural and environmental sensitivity, the expanse of the project alone posed challenges that tested every fibre of my professional being. But it also offered opportunities that few in my shoes could dream of.

Site visits spanned two entire days, not counting the three-hour drive from Mumbai. With no running water, electricity or internet, even basic communication was a challenge. We needed to create our own infrastructure from the ground up. Before we could lay a single brick, there were roads to be built and makeshift lodgings for the hundreds of workers who would be onsite for months, if not years. Every element that is typically taken for granted in urban construction became a hurdle. We didn't stop for a moment. Water was sourced from nearby natural springs and treated onsite. We installed generators and solar panels to supply power. And for communication, we even resorted to old-school walkie-talkies, which surprisingly became an effective tool in the vastness of the land.

Cultural sensitivity was another aspect of the project that didn't make it to any blueprint. The region was home to indigenous communities whose lives, livelihoods and heritage had to be respected. We got them involved in the project, employing local artisans and workers, ensuring the estate not only provided economic opportunities but also a place that truly celebrated local art and culture. In turn we gained a predictable labour force and built a community of people that would preserve the land for generations to come.

One of our greatest challenges was sourcing materials efficiently. The terrain was unsuitable for large, heavily loaded trucks, necessitating multiple trips with smaller vehicles, which escalated costs. We realigned the designs to incorporate locally sourced material; this not only reduced our carbon footprint and supply chain costs but infused the essence of the locale into every corner of the estate.

We had no room for second-guessing; indecision would have been a luxury we couldn't afford. *Am I doing enough? Is this the right path?* These questions became moot. Instead, our focus was entirely on what needed to be done next with what we knew now.

Faced with the task of planning sewage treatment for one hundred hotel rooms spread out over 300 acres, the limitations of traditional wastewater systems became immediately evident. Such systems would necessitate an intricate network of pipes stretching over a hundred miles, a solution that was both inefficient and potentially fraught with issues, especially if gradient inconsistencies required the addition of submersible pumps. Seeking a more effective and sustainable alternative, we stumbled upon soil biofiltration technology. This innovation allowed us to equip each room with its own small waste filtration unit, which converted waste into manure for enriching the soil and produced greywater suitable for irrigating the surrounding flora.

While the stories are endless, over the years, the estate transformed from a blueprint into an architectural masterpiece, and more importantly, a hub for cultural and environmental conservation. It stands as a testament to the power of action – adaptive, relentless and resolute.

The inescapable truth to any business, as in life, is that uncertainty is the only certainty there is. The good news is that we innately hold the adaptive capacity essential for thriving amidst this dynamism. Through deliberate adaptive action, we have the power to transform these uncertainties into incredible avenues for unprecedented growth. Adaptive action can help seamlessly bridge aspiration and accomplishment where our dreams cease to be just fleeting thoughts but future realities in the making.

Occasionally, the unpredictable landscape of the construction industry graces us with rare yet powerful moments of absolute clarity – unveiling a unique opportunity where the path is clear and decisive action yields specific, predictable outcomes. It is a confluence where years of your unique experience, knowledge and instinct align with a fleeting window of golden opportunity that almost flirtatiously invites swift, impactful action. For me, these illuminated moments of lucid certainty are where massive action, supercharged with conviction and purpose, become the silent architects of success, quietly orchestrating moments of undeniable brilliance amidst chaos and uncertainty.

ABOUT KEZYA DE BRAGANÇA

Kezya De Bragança's career has spanned two decades of contributions to India's real estate and construction sectors. As the founder and CEO of Bettamint Technologies, Kezya is leading the digital transformation of frontline workforce management in construction, placing a significant emphasis on streamlining digital payments and promoting financial inclusion for the sector's underserved demographics.

Concurrently, she serves as executive director at Riviera Constructions, pioneers in shaping Goa's real estate and hospitality sectors with a legacy spanning over thirty years.

In 2018, Kezya founded MansionHaus, a luxury boutique hotel and impact club restored within a three-hundred-year-old heritage mansion. MansionHaus has garnered numerous awards and gained recognition as one of Time *magazine's 'Worlds' 100 Greatest Places' in 2021.*

Prior to her current endeavours, Kezya held leadership roles within large organisations like Prestige Group, Hilton Worldwide India and Writer Corporation, where she scaled portfolios of real estate developments in India in excess of $1.2 billion across varied asset classes and markets.

One of her most notable achievements was the development of the 3,500 acre Shillim Valley, a UNESCO World Heritage Site, into the highly acclaimed Hilton Shillim Estate Retreat & Spa, also known as Dharana Retreat.

Don't forget that it's through and with people that you'll experience some of the greatest achievements available to you. Yes, yes, you've heard that it's a people industry – that's great, but what are you doing with it? Are you genuinely committed to expanding your horizon of possibilities or are you only seeing who is available to you at arm's length and wanting the best of the best to come to you? It's rare to meet people in the industry who are more interested in the possibility of the relationship than the immediate transaction, and one of those people is exemplary leader, David Privitera. People remain the greatest complexity of them all, but David has been able to simply get it right. How? Let's see …

8

BUILDING RELATIONSHIPS

BY DAVID M PRIVITERA

WHAT IS ONE THING YOU WOULD TELL A PERSON?

Who you surround yourself with is one of the most important decisions you'll ever make.

WHY?

As you progress through your career and chart your path forward, it becomes evident that the road to success is filled with others also trying to navigate their own pathways. When you have a group of people working together, and you rely on the strength and quality of your relationships to reach your goals, the results tend to be more profound and fulfilling for each person involved. You quickly learn that with the collaboration and support of others, everyone achieves greater success.

Life and business coach Tony Robbins notably said, 'The quality of your life is in direct proportion to the quality of your relationships.' You can apply this same sage advice to the achievements in your construction career. That success will be in direct proportion to the quality of your relationships.

When I started my career in the construction industry, I would have never anticipated the impact and importance of my relationships with clients, colleagues and coworkers. After I began to lead and grow my own organisation, the dynamic of the employer/employee relationship also proved to be one of the most critical aspects to nurture and strengthen.

In recent years, I started to recognise consistent attributes in my own relationships and identified some personal core principles relating to whom I spent time with and where I found success and growth in doing so. While these ideas are not original, when applied together, your relationships can have a profound impact on your personal and professional growth:

- Begin with the goal of surrounding yourself with only the best people to support and challenge you in the right way. This will lead to better collaboration, effective constructive feedback and a diversity of ideas. Think of it as 'building a smart room'.
- Practise humility and learn to flex your empathy muscles! Building and nurturing relationships includes care and compassion for others.
- Create meaningful experiences for those around you. People will remember who and what helped them to where they are now and how they were treated along the way.

IT STARTS (AND ENDS) WITH TRUST

When you choose to pursue a career in the construction industry, regardless of what stage you are at, not only do you get to participate and build important projects, but equally significant, you get the chance to create and nurture amazing relationships. The heart of these relationships is built on trust.

Trust forms the core of any successful relationship. It serves as the foundation upon which cooperation, effective communication and mutual respect are formed. In an industry known for its complexity and inherent risks, establishing and maintaining trust is critical for achieving success.

Construction projects involve multiple stakeholders with diverse interests, ranging from owners and contractors to architects, engineers and vendors. Trust allows these stakeholders to overcome potential conflicts and work towards a common goal. It enables open and honest communication, encourages information sharing and promotes collective decision-making. When trust is present, everyone involved is more likely to rely on each other's expertise, delegate responsibilities and work together to tackle problems, ultimately leading to better results.

Transparent communication is a basic ingredient for building trust. Transparency in sharing progress, risks and challenges helps build trust by fostering a sense of shared responsibility. A regular cadence of discussions encourages open dialogue, provides opportunities for clarifications and promotes trust among team members.

Beyond professional interactions, building personal relationships helps foster trust among stakeholders. Engaging in informal conversations, team-building activities and social events cultivates a sense of camaraderie and a personal bond. When individuals know and trust each other on a personal level, it tends to promote better communication, empathy and cooperation. Creating opportunities for personal connections builds rapport and contributes to a more harmonious working environment.

Ultimately, trust is built and maintained when the people around you consistently deliver on their promises and meet expectations. This includes fulfilling your obligations, meeting all milestones and delivering high-quality work throughout the process. When team members consistently demonstrate their reliability, it builds confidence and establishes a culture of trust. In contrast, failing to deliver on commitments will erode trust and can have significant consequences not only for a project's success, but also on your personal and professional reputation.

By prioritising collaboration, trust and effective communication, you can navigate the complexities of the construction business, drive successful outcomes and continue to grow your leadership skills throughout your career on the pillars of strong relationships. The benefits of strong relationships extend beyond individual projects. They create opportunities for long-term partnerships, reputational growth and business expansion. Even as the industry continues to evolve, if you recognise the profound impact of your relationships and commit to cultivating a culture that reinforces their importance, you vastly increase your probability of success.

SURROUND YOURSELF NOT ONLY WITH GREAT PEOPLE, BUT THE RIGHT PEOPLE

By now you should start to see a pattern: trust and relationships play a fundamental role in the context of surrounding yourself with great people. Beyond that, it is equally important to be certain that they are the *right people* for your team.

Here are some key reasons why it is essential:

- **Diverse skill sets:** You cannot excel in every aspect of your company or projects. Having a team with complementary skills allows you to tackle challenges from different angles and promotes innovation. The right people can fuel each other's creativity, leading to innovative solutions and new ideas.
- **Improved decision-making and productivity:** When you have a team of intelligent and experienced individuals, they can contribute unique perspectives and insights. This diversity of thought leads to more informed and well-rounded decision-making processes. They inspire and push each other to perform at their best, leading to increased efficiency and productivity.
- **Faster problem-solving:** The right team of people can effectively address problems and obstacles as they arise. With a wealth of experience and knowledge, the team can identify potential obstacles and consequences more quickly, minimising any setbacks.
- **Learning and growth:** Working with talented individuals provides a continuous educational opportunity. Collaborating with them allows you to gain new knowledge and perspectives, contributing to both your personal and professional growth.
- **Stronger culture:** Positive and high-performing individuals

contribute to a healthy company culture. A strong culture fosters loyalty, commitment and a sense of purpose.

- **Increased credibility and reputation:** When your business and projects are associated with exceptional people with proven track records, it enhances your credibility and reputation in the industry. This can have a compounding effect on finding and retaining other great people as part of the team.

- **Resilience in challenging times:** When facing tough times, the right people can provide the support needed to weather any storm. They will band together, offer unique perspectives and find innovative ways to navigate and remove any obstacle.

Simply put, surrounding yourself with talented people is clearly important, but surrounding yourself with the *right people* is a game changer.

FINDING THE RIGHT ONES

Building relationships, whether in business or personal life, is a key aspect to growth and success in your professional endeavours. That said, before you can truly build any relationship, you need to put yourself in surroundings conducive to meeting people that can help nurture your growth, goals and expand your circle of influence.

I have found that my most meaningful relationships have come from a collection of places and perspectives. There are obvious paths including industry colleagues, networking events and trade-related organisations. In recent years, I have focused on meeting peers that are involved in businesses of similar size and geography, but with no involvement in the construction industry.

Through these experiences, I have discovered unique views and problem-solving approaches that have allowed me to expand my decision-making skills. In return, I always try to create a positive and supportive environment where both parties can thrive and grow together.

CALCULATE YOUR RETURN ON RELATIONSHIPS

The idea of a return on relationships (ROR), as coined by social marketing strategist Ted Rubin, requires deliberate effort and commitment. Strategies such as early engagement, personal rapport and a track record of successful collaborations contribute to cultivating trust among stakeholders. By investing in relationship-building efforts, construction professionals can secure repeat business, foster client satisfaction and unlock opportunities for innovation and growth. This can lead to a significant compounding of your ROR!

As construction professionals, we must embrace a culture of continuous improvement and learn from experiences. Analysing past projects, capturing lessons learned and implementing best practices contributes to the evolution of relationship-driven approaches in the industry. This culture of improvement not only enhances project performance but also adds to the overall results, growth and advancement of your business and the people in it.

A SIMPLE CONCLUSION

All relationships must have a give and take. You need to make yourself available and be willing to support others even if there isn't an immediate benefit to you or your construction career and business. Remain empathetic, humble and genuine. Be the type of person that you look for in a relationship.

If what you have read thus far hasn't made it profoundly evident, let me close with this reference.

In an eighty-year long Harvard University Study of Adult Development, the longest study on human happiness ever completed, it came to a simple and profound conclusion: good relationships lead to more happiness and better health.

In other words, take care of your important relationships, and they will take care of you.

ABOUT DAVID PRIVITERA

David Privitera is the president and CEO of Concorde Construction Company, headquartered in Charlotte, NC, USA.

He started his career in the construction industry in 1990, and over the last three decades has developed a reputation as an admired leader known for his strategic vision, leadership acumen and unwavering commitment to excellence.

David's leadership approach centres around empowering team members, fostering a culture of accountability and nurturing professional growth.

David joined Concorde Construction in 2005 as executive vice president and managing partner, giving the company a springboard for greater growth. His focus was to establish a successful culture and cultivate strategic customer relationships. In 2011, David was named president and in 2016 was given the added role of CEO.

In the following years, David transformed Concorde Construction into a respected general contractor and construction management firm with completed projects valued at more than $1 billion throughout the south-eastern United States.

Outside of work, he is dedicated to giving back to his community through philanthropy and mentorship opportunities, embodying his commitment to contributing to the greater good and leaving a lasting positive impact.

I reflect on a time I was railroaded by senior management incompetency and how I was stunned into silence. First, that this practice was around, and second, at management's ability to have a scrappy skill set when it comes to the delicate practice of providing feedback that has fact not fiction, substance over opinion and so on. And I wasn't the only one who faced this, experiencing many distraught mentees coming back from the battlefield of incompetent management. This next principle cannot be taken seriously enough, as shared by Elvin K Box, for it could wholly change the dynamics and experiences of many in the industry if applied in its totality ...

9

THE POWERFUL CONSEQUENCE OF DELIVERING FEEDBACK CONSTRUCTIVELY

BY ELVIN K. BOX

WHAT IS ONE THING YOU WOULD TELL A PERSON?

Develop your knowledge, skills and ability in delivering constructive feedback.

WHY?

Just like in team sports, construction projects have young rookies with raw, undeveloped talent and high levels of enthusiasm. These young, dedicated and maturing professionals need guidance to steer them towards good, solid managerial practice. All to boost their careers and, whilst working on your project, for them to be as efficient and effective as possible. This is why constructive feedback is imperative, as each manager or leader who is instilled with the responsibility of delivering feedback can make or break another's career.

Not forgetting the skilful delivery of constructive feedback continually improves a manager's emotional intelligence, which psychologist Daniel Goleman popularised as being crucial for effective leadership. A point I shall elaborate upon within this chapter. How pivotal of a skill this is, yet nearly everyone in the industry can attest to experiences where feedback delivered was underwhelming at best. In all your professional practices, who has taught you the micro and macro consequences of feedback delivery? Are you aware of its impact on mental health, performance and culture, all intricately interwoven to the fabric of how feedback is delivered?

However, throughout my career I have generally, save for one exceptional encounter, endured 'non-feedback'. On one unfortunately highly memorable occasion, I received an extremely critical opinion of my performance.

It was delivered without a thought for the impact it was having upon my self-confidence and motivation. No mention was made of how I might improve my performance, nor any mention made of where I was performing well.

Most importantly, it was devoid of an opportunity for me to offer an opinion on what I perceived I had done well, nor the invitation to explain what I might do differently next time. Basically, it was a diatribe, thinly disguised as a 'performance review'.

Unfortunately, this is still the way on many construction

projects. There are far too many managers who are solely results orientated and oblivious of the importance professional development has to the people who report to them whilst on their project.

Such managers give orders, often less than impressed with the results, yet not working with their staff to reflect upon their staff's performance. This would ensure the individual improves and the project gains from the ensuing lessons learnt. And, of course, the managers miss out on developing their own emotional intelligence. Hence, the reliability of this method of developing high performers and high-performing project teams sits squarely on the shoulders of the manager delivering it.

WHAT TO CONSIDER WHEN DELIVERING CONSTRUCTIVE FEEDBACK

Managers should ensure the feedback is specific, enabling the person to know what they have achieved and what they need to do to improve and/or progress further. Formally or informally, the feedback should never just be an evaluative statement like, 'Well done,' or, 'That's great, you nailed it!' This doesn't tell the person what was done well or what was great about it.

To be reliable, constructive feedback should feature specific facts which relate to progress or achievement, to focus the person on a specific element of their development. Consequently, the powerful consequence is they know what specifically needs developing and what is currently missing. Also, why it is deficient and how it can be improved. Likewise, a similar narrative will be shared on the individual's achievements.

Such constructive feedback is the bedrock of personal

development, as you are simultaneously identifying what lean construction philosophy terms the 'waste of underutilised, or mismatched, employee skill sets'. Constructive feedback checks performance evaluations for issues and seeks to avoid cost of underperforming or, of course, underused skills. Ultimately ensuring employees can perform to the best of their abilities.

The golden rule I have learnt when delivering constructive feedback is to explain what you observed and what you heard. Consequently, your constructive feedback focuses you specifically on the person's behaviours and not their character traits. Hence you shall use more 'verbs' than 'adjectives'.

For example, instead of feeding back, 'Your antics with the subcontractor's supervisor were like that of a wildly aggressive dervish,' the feedback should be, 'You replied in a loud voice and repeatedly interrupted the subcontractor's supervisor.'

The person receiving the feedback shall recognise that this is true, heartfelt and considerate constructive feedback. Its intent is positive and could never be construed as an attack on their personality. The person will feel reassured, guided and supported.

From my own experience, I recall being an up-and-coming construction project manager and seconded to a large railway resignalling project. I was appraised by the project director, a highly experienced, well-respected and eminently professional civil engineer. He fed back my clear progression of successfully transferring my knowledge and skills, developed on commercial construction projects, and adapting them to railway engineering. Specifically, how my area of the project had made significant progress against the program.

Yet, with great empathy and exceptional social skills, he

explained that to sustain this excellent professional development I must communicate operational deficiencies to supervisors in a composed manner, with clarity, and seek confirmation my feedback has been understood and appreciated.

It was exemplary constructive feedback, because significantly it concluded with an opportunity for me to explain what I did or did not agree with and, most importantly, why?

HOW CONSTRUCTIVE FEEDBACK RAISES AND SUSTAINS PERFORMANCE

It is a must to review your people's progress regularly, and that is not just 'annually'. Each review will produce items that should be reviewed in a timely period, commensurate with the improvement required. This may require a particular review every three months, or possibly a monthly basis, if the subordinate is particularly struggling in one aspect of their performance.

This gives you the opportunity, through constructive feedback, to discuss on a one-to-one basis, the three cornerstones of personal growth that underpin raising and sustaining a construction professional's performance:

1. How they are **progressing.**
2. What they have **achieved**.
3. What they need to **improve.**

Everyone needs to know how they are progressing in their career, what they have achieved and what fell short of the mark. Without such constructive feedback, this vital information would not be attainable.

Constructive feedback provides opportunities for the person to make any adjustments or improvements required to not only reach a particular standard, but very importantly encourage them to embark on a lifelong journey of continuous improvement.

The key elements of constructive feedback, and how they raise and sustain performance, are hallmarked by the following:

- ✓ It was actioned in a timely manner and specific in content.
- ✓ Created opportunities for clarification and discussion.
- ✓ The emphasis was on progress as opposed to failure.
- ✓ It enabled the person to know what they have achieved.
- ✓ The individual was invited to offer suggestions on how they felt they performed, improvements they would make and how they would do things differently.
- ✓ The individual can state what, and why, they were in disagreement with any of the feedback.
- ✓ The improvement in the person's confidence and motivation were tangible.
- ✓ Further learning opportunities, or any action required, were clearly highlighted, clarified and where necessary timebound.

They should most definitely walk away from your feedback session with the following in abundance:

- Their confidence boosted.
- Encouraged to continually improve.
- Motivated to attain and maintain resilience.

ACKNOWLEDGED BEST PRACTISE METHODS AND APPROACHES TO DELIVER CONSTRUCTIVE FEEDBACK

The person delivering feedback has to ensure heightened awareness to more than just the words they are saying when communicating your feedback, so that your words are in complete harmony with your:

- Body language (specifically active, engaged listening).
- Facial expressions (specifically eye-to-eye contact).
- Tone of voice (specifically avoid monotone).

If the person hears first what they have done well, this should be followed by what they need to improve and then end on a positive note to ensure they retain their motivation. This is commonly known as the 'praise sandwich'.

The ideal praise-to-criticism ratio, as cited by clinical psychologist Aubery Daniels, is that 'high performers' are expected to react best to three positives to one negative. However, for the average person it is often deemed to be four to one.

Now, very importantly, when undertaking behavioural management of safety as a consultant, we were urged to consider sitting, or standing, shoulder to shoulder with the people we were delivering constructive feedback to. This enabled our discussion to be focused on what we had written or drawn on a slip of paper, or perhaps a whiteboard. This ensured we drew attention to the paper, or whiteboard, and did not address any individuals directly, face-to-face.

Symbolically, we were talking about the feedback and not any individual person. This removed as much emotion as possible from the act of constructive feedback. It was in no way personal, as it was addressing only information. A positive outcome is that people did hear what we wanted them to hear, and they were more than happy to continue discussing the issues in a collaborative manner.

WHY YOU MUST DEVELOP ADVANCED EMOTIONAL INTELLIGENCE

Constructive feedback, when delivered with aplomb, enhances the emotional intelligence of the manager delivering the feedback. Emotional intelligence is often cited as the central plank to enhancing the delivering of feedback, which considers the following:

- **Empathy:** caring for others' feelings by 'standing in their shoes' when feeding back.
- **Social skills:** enabling excellent communication skills and trusting rapport is quickly generated before, during and after the feedback.
- **Self-awareness:** recognition of your emotions and their triggers, specifically during a feedback session.
- **Self-regulation:** able to take a step back during a feedback session to converse in the most efficient and effective way possible.
- **Motivation:** able to motivate both themselves and, very importantly, others. During a feedback session, adjust responses to guide individuals towards positive outcome and goals.

FINAL THOUGHTS

With practise, and of course appropriate training and coaching, the above stated advice in this chapter will become second nature. Managers will become adroit at reliable constructive feedback, because it will embody the framework that UNC Kenan-Flagler Business School Professor Elad Sherf recommends – 'the 3Cs':

• Provides transparent direction (**clarity**).
• Emphasises employees' goals (**contextual meaning**).
• Negotiates employees' affective reactions (**composure**).

Sherf recommends using this framework as a guide for turning every constructive feedback session into an opportunity to demonstrate empathy and help employees achieve lasting growth, learning and improvement.

ABOUT ELVIN K. BOX MCIOB MBA

An apprentice carpenter and joiner with renowned London builders, Holloway White Allom, Elvin qualified as a chartered builder and commenced working as a construction manager with major construction consultants on high-profile projects, such as The Langham, London, one of the world's most iconic luxury hotels.

Attaining an MBA with the Open University Business School, Elvin immediately commenced tutoring on their MBA program. Specifically, creativity, innovation and change, which led to working for global construction consultancy Mace, on behavioural management and innovation assignments.

Now an independent consultant and international keynote speaker, plus chair of Constructing Excellence's London Club, has led to Elvin's involvement with two construction industry improvement assignments: the UK government's 'National Digital Twin programme' (NDTp), digital transformation of infrastructure and construction and member of the committee tasked to produce and disseminate BS 99001:2022, a QMS standard that builds on ISO 9001 to radically improve its application across the built environment.

What do you really, really, really want? How closely do you examine and reorient your North Star to ensure that where you choose to walk remains relevant? Imagine getting into a car and never knowing your destination. Imagine going on a hike but not marking where the pinnacle is. It's not hard to imagine; this is how most people run their career and lives. And then you have someone who so consciously and with precise intent seeks to not leave success to chance. This is Robert Penney, an industry leader whose rare results demonstrate that there was no accident to success. How? Here's exactly how.

10

Defining Success

BY ROBERT J PENNEY

WHAT IS ONE THING YOU WOULD TELL A PERSON?

If you first define success, the path to achieve it becomes clear.

WHY?

The case can be made that there is no other industry that relies more heavily on the proper cooperation and collaboration of individuals with vastly different skill sets and from more diverse backgrounds than the construction industry. Each day, we bring to life the design of the architect, get one step closer to the vision of the owner, admire the skills of the craft turning materials into structure and watch the symphony orchestra that is a construction project conducted by a contractor. This is the essence of what makes the construction industry rich, vibrant and lively.

Yet, as with our own lives, the complexity that brings beauty and meaning also brings competing interests. Should we work longer today? Spend time with friends and family? Start a new book? Exercise? Catch up on sleep? Or take time off? All options that will enrich our lives, but the choice is what makes it complex and at times paralysing. What do you choose?

This manifests in our work. Do we complete the task faster or take longer and produce a more quality product? Which brings more value – the speed or the quality of the work? Or do neither matter and only the cost does? Or in fact do none of them trump performing the work safely? The lack of clarity around what success truly means, about what the *definition of success* actually is, is the root of the problem.

The meaningful wisdom that is found here, that has the ability to transform a person's life both professionally and personally, *is that if you first define success, the path to achieve it becomes clear.*

On the most successful construction projects I have been a part of, the one common thread is that the teams had a clear aligned vision of where they were going. All of these high-**performing** teams varied greatly in their execution and styles of work, but the definition of success in their minds was clear. They all knew the direction they were running in.

> 'He who has a why can bear almost any how.'
> – *Friedrich Nietzsche*

This clear understanding that if I can get this request for information answered to ensure the design intent is maintained while we pour the concrete slab in what will be the owners' jewel box lobby entrance and the first sight that the public will see when they walk in – this is what changes meaningless work to a meaningful career. Understanding what we are really doing.

Data entry, endless meetings and long hours without reason is demoralising, uninspiring and not sustainable. Yet, toiling on hard problems where you cannot get the idea out of your head, you have to write, work through it aloud with others and rejoice when you solve it and see it come to life – that is inspiring. Why?

It is the same amount of work. Actually, the inspiring almost always requires more work than the uninspiring. Yet we feel energised and enthusiastic. The reason is the understanding of success. The defined goal of where we are headed. The fruits of the labour that could bear if we only can get there.

UNVEILING THE SECRET

The one thing I would tell a person, to hope to transfer what has undoubtedly changed my life and could do the same for them, is how to define success. The two tools I use both personally and professionally are:

1. **Learn to properly define success** – conditions of satisfaction.
2. **Succeed daily** – find the successes every day and highlight them.

The first core concept is to learn how to properly define success. Conditions of satisfaction is an exercise that can be performed on yourself, with a small or large group. I perform them in-person, but also virtually if need be. The concept is to understand for a given circumstance, what are the conditions of the outcome that would mean success. For this example, I will use a simple scenario: A workshop. You are meeting with a group of five people who are putting on a workshop in a month for fifty people and they need help understanding how to do it. We first will sit down and say, 'At the end of the workshop and it is all wrapped up, what would it look like if it went successfully? Be specific.' Give the team five to ten minutes to write these conditions on sticky notes. After time has passed, have each individual share their notes out loud.

It had a clear agenda.

Everyone had a chance to speak.

The participants enjoyed it. We tried fun breakout groups.

The food has to be good. I always remember the meetings with bad food.

Breaks, we need breaks. And need to control individuals who talk over others.

We created a clear list of action items.

We have planned meetings moving forward to work on our goals.

As the ideas start coming in, I put them on a flip chart/whiteboard/virtual screen. I will prompt the individuals, do any others have a condition like this? In the example above, you'll see 'everyone has a voice' and 'control people who talk over others' are related. We will group them together. Slowly, but surely, your board will fill up to the brim. You will have a clear list of what a successful workshop looks like and what you need to do. Create a clear agenda, design breaks in it, ensure the room has food and is comfortable, include exercises that allow all voices to be heard, don't leave the room without an action item list.

Getting conditions of satisfaction seems so simple and at times trivial. That's the point. That is what success is.

'Success is the sum of small efforts, repeated day-in and day-out.' – Robert Collier

'Life is really simple, but we insist on making it complicated.' – Confucius

Imagine if every aspect of your work – meetings, projects, your development, your team's development, your new ideas – had a clear set of conditions that, if met, you would achieve success and you merely need to execute on those basic items.

After learning how to properly define success, the second life-changing tool is to bring success into your life every day and announce it. All the meetings I run start with a clear statement of success.

'Good morning, team, it's 11am and we are meeting for ninety minutes today to talk about how we onboard new team members. We will have a five-minute break at the forty-five-minute mark. For today, we are only focusing on the new hire orientation, and we will leave all other aspects of it for our next call. How's that sound?'

The meeting has been kicked off with simple, clear parameters. The team knows what we are talking about, for how long, how the meeting will go and when we will talk about additional items. As the meeting finishes:

'Great meeting, today's team. We worked through the entire new hire orientation process. We decided on an 80% plan that all new hires will be onboarded through and left 20% to be customised for the project and office. We will communicate the plan to leadership by the end of month and communicate the response afterwards.'

The meeting is finished with the clear statement of what was talked about, what is happening next and the value the individuals who spent their time in your meeting gave. This is what it means to succeed daily.

IMPACT AND IMPLICATIONS

This is what it means to define success, detail the path to get there, and execute the steps slowly and surely. A day is made up of hours, a week is made up of days, a month is made up of weeks, a year is made up of months.

The construction of the world's most breathtaking structures from the Sydney Opera House, Sagrada Familia, to the Empire State Building were the compounded result of deliveries of material to the site, the successful placement of a brick, the small iterative meetings around specific elements, repeated over and over again. Until one day, the result was achieved, success obtained, the world forever changed, and through the process you will be forever changed as well.

'Be regular and orderly in your life, so that you may be violent and original in your work.' – Gustave Flaubert

PERSONAL INSIGHT AND REFLECTIONS

If we first define success, the path to achieve it becomes clear. While writing this chapter, I defined success as conveying a simple tool based on my life experience that has changed my life for the better in a way that the reader could put down this book and go put it into practice immediately. To convey a concept that so much of the difficulty we experience in life is merely the lack of clarity on direction and not understanding the 'why' less than it is the actual work and difficulty in life itself.

CONCLUSION

Take the time to pause and define what success looks like for yourself, for your work and for others. Base your actions moving forward off this clearer purpose and watch the ripples of positive impact it creates in your life. But most importantly, do it every day. Celebrate your wins and the wins of others around you. That's what will define a successful life.

ABOUT ROBERT PENNEY

Rob Penney is the national director of continuous improvement for Skanska. A certified six sigma black belt, advanced lean certified practitioner and SAFe agilest, Rob has spent sixteen years in the construction industry including a decade in field operations with Skanska. Rob currently leads the National Continuous Improvement Committee (NCIC), a twenty-member team of lean and agile experts and facilitators who create a culture of continuous improvement in the field and in offices around the globe. As a thought leader, Rob speaks frequently on high-performing team creation, operational excellence and continuous improvement. Rob is based in Philadelphia, Pennsylvania, a graduate of Drexel University with certification from Villanova University and the Virginia Mason Institute.

Introducing the first young gun to the anthology, Heimy Lee Libu Molina. Someone whose influence, results and early successes remain an anomaly in a sea of sameness and mediocrity. When most people have an allergic reaction to building tediously, imperfectly and diligently, Heimy has been able to construct her career in a way that creates solid foundations for whatever comes next. Her career to date wasn't a chance collision of events, but rather a strategy that when applied, will always see you moving in on opportunities that the rest of the industry is sleeping to. Has Heimy revealed how she developed her championship mindset? Discover it for yourself.

11

BRICK BY BRICK

BY HEIMY LEE LIBU MOLINA

WHAT IS ONE THING YOU WOULD TELL A PERSON?

To build a perfect wall, you must start laying one brick perfectly at a time.

WHY?

The atmosphere seems intimidating from ground level – a mountain would always seem astronomical when you look at its tip; skyscrapers appear enormous when looking from street level. A university degree seems lengthy if you're just starting; a million dollars may seem unattainable if you're starting with a dollar – everything seems daunting when you're at the starting line. Yet they all stand tall, grand, in front of you, complete in their monumental nature. Consider these like a brick wall – a brick wall would seem colossal at first, but in hindsight, it's just an object that's made up of smaller, quantifiable bricks. So, to build your dreams, you must begin by the execution of one idea, one action, one move after another. To successfully build a brick wall, you must start laying it brick by brick. How else do you think things that are larger than life are built? How does your inner David encounter the Goliaths of your life?

I'm a person of ambition from an early age. In the early stages of my life, I have always felt the need to overachieve. I quickly became insecure and kept comparing myself to famous young achievers and to my acquaintances who'd accomplished immensely at such a young age – I was envious. With this jealousy, I'd created a list of goals. Although the essence of listing out goals is harmless, the root cause of it wasn't. It made me become hungrier for outrageous goals that I had no way of knowing how to attain. I desired these goals so I would look triumphant, just like the others. They made it look so effortless, so I thought these successes required no effort to accomplish. As expected, I ended up not acquiring these desired accolades. The reasons being: (1) The desire to accomplish was rooted from a place of hate; (2) I kept trying to take huge, unsustainable leaps to get what I want – I thought that only the big milestones mattered; and (3) I didn't take any small steps towards my goal. I thought Rome could be built in a day. And then it hit me – the only way to build my own monumental career and life is to lay a single brick daily without fail.

Like many other things, getting into this philosophy was no easy feat. I didn't build the 'brick by brick' principle in one go – like the principle, it was an incremental process. It was elicited by a chain reaction of the various, well-thought choices and proactive actions I have done in my life. If this mentality didn't become my ethos, my bio could be summed up in two words – Heimy existed – and this mediocrity-filled description didn't bode well with me. Without this mentality, I would not have been an award recipient, podcast guest, article subject, guest speaker, committee member and much more. Without this mentality, I would've been mediocre.

Remember, small steps can take you anywhere, *but taking no steps gets you nowhere* – an idea without execution will forever remain as a wish. Every year, I create a vision board for myself that is in line with what person I want to become in a year's time frame. This is focused on the final output, the big picture, the version of Heimy that I want to become. However, what drives this into fruition is the daily grind, the day-to-day actions that move towards the path to completion. It's the small steps that will compound into the bigger picture of my goal. The goals I have achieved were the compounding effect of every single brainstorming session, mentoring opportunity, intensive research, hard decision and delayed gratification that I have done throughout my journey. Every small sacrifice amounted to monumental rewards. Small wins are usually underappreciated due to the nature of its size of impact. Although these types of wins are insignificant at first, the destination will not be attained without their presence. Big wins inspire us to achieve more, but small wins are what keeps us going despite struggles. Never underestimate the power of small wins. You're conditioned to take small wins towards project outcomes, have you considered the same for yourself? *Harvard Business Review's* 'The Power of Small Wins' (2011) highlighted the importance of incremental progress in goal achievement. In their research, the minor steps taken by the subjects evoked an outsized positive reaction to their work and resulted in a triumphant milestone. Like many other things, a key part of building your wall is the journey. Everything is a process. So, if you take each goal into one process at a time, each wall into one brick at a time, you'll be more likely to build your desired brick wall at the end.

I'm aware that attaining small wins to get to the big wins is easier said than done. Like in buildings, procurement comes first before the construction process. In this case, you must seek your 'bricks' in life before you can start creating your wall. Bricks don't simply fall in your lap – you must actively seek your bricks to obtain the ones suitable for your wall, as not all kinds of bricks would have a place in it. You must have the right mindset and aligned values before you commence building your wall, in actioning your goal, which looks like:

- **Starting from scratch, wherein you need to acquire the raw materials to make the bricks.** You may currently not have the right skill set for your goal, but a dull pencil can always be sharpened.
- **Or the bricks have been previously broken, and you must put them together before you start to build.** If adapted principles have been forgotten or there is a need to 'unlearn' certain anomalies, it is never too late to realign your vision and forge a better path.
- **In some cases, the bricks are just lying there for you to grab – all you have to do is take action!**

To achieve the optimum results of the bricklaying principle, you must act on the following:

- **Discipline** – the act of delaying gratification.
- **Diligence** – the act of ceasing all signs of surrender.
- **Consistency** – the act of small wins.
- **Velocity** – the act of advancing to a direction.
- **Achievement** – the act of goal accomplishment.

The person that you are now and the person that you want to be are separated by this fine line called discipline. The gap between thinking and doing are bridged by this thing called the 'first step' – the first brick. This step will be the hardest step to take and the most courageous one you'll ever perform. I have always admired great writers, but I thought I'd never be one, until it hit me – the only reason that I am not a great writer is that I have never written a book, let alone a chapter. The mere thought of pouring my views into writing scared me and I became surrounded with 'what-ifs'. And instead of that fear overtaking my desire to write, I used that fear to fuel the fire that is my vision of becoming a compelling writer. With this fear, I took my first step and wrote my first paragraphs.

With discipline comes diligence. Struggles are inevitable in life, and these exist either to: (a) create chaos and derail your journey or (b) come out stronger on the other side – what dictates the result is your choice. At the age of nineteen, I packed my bags and flew to Australia to pursue engineering overseas. This new chapter filled me with excitement for the voyage ahead, as moving away from home was a rite of passage for me. This milestone symbolises not only independence, but also a chance to flourish at an international level. But with this excitement came fear – the fear of not being good enough in comparison to domestic students. With this, I had a choice: to choose fear or to choose diligence. Since I wanted to come out stronger on the other side, I actively chose diligence in everything that I did. A difficult unit? Study hard. New to the country? Meet people. Network. A different language? Immerse. Converse. A big degree to finish? Graduate with flying colours. After choosing diligence over fear, for multiple times, one after the other, it became second nature to me. With diligence, I tirelessly and courageously worked on the life that I have built – myself.

Once you've set a goal, you've already laid the first brick and have committed yourself to a learning journey that will lead you to your brick wall – your vision. Goal-setting builds your foundation, but the consistency of taking action and generating small wins will bring you closer to constructing your brick wall. These small wins will induce a 'compounding effect' towards your main goal. The compounding effect, in this instance, is the collective ability of your actions, both past and present, in producing desired outcomes in relation to your goal. Like compounding interest, the compounding effect of each brick laid (your actions) will result in the construction of your brick wall (goals) at an efficient rate. The 'brick by brick' message is a collective product of my experiences. I didn't acquire all the accolades that I have by just doing one thing. I consistently strived to show my commitment to my career enhancement and personal brand through my day-to-day actions. Without those consistencies, my brick wall would not have been built.

Building your wall at a faster rate will amount to nothing if the direction is not in line with your ethos. Basic physics taught us that speed with direction is velocity. But now, I will teach you how the speed and direction of velocity is an important facet of your life-building journey. The consistency of laying one brick at a time is deemed worthless if each brick is not laid with the intention of progressing towards a specified endpoint at a certain calibre of excellence, in an achievable time frame. At the 2023 Engineers Australia Winter Ball, I was one of two masters of ceremony – my first opportunity to be an emcee of a well-renowned event. This was no feat of chance or luck, this was a chain reaction of all awards, participations, volunteering and proactive choices I have made. If the direction of my previous actions does not point to my desired end goal, then there was no purpose to those actions. If the brick you're laying is not a brick that contributes to the wall that you're building, why lay it? Why hinder progress? Why delay the feeling of achievement?

Achievement is the triumphant completion of your brick-laying journey. This signifies the end to this journey but the start of several possibilities. In the span of a lifetime, you'll naturally want to build more than one wall, achieve more than one goal. So let this ultimate milestone of achievement be the start of your prohibition towards fragmentary goals and spark the fire of establishing success.

Do you want to live your best life by being the best version of yourself? Do it brick by brick.

Whether your wall signifies your university journey, a new-found career path or a health goal – you can build it, as long as you start laying one brick at a time.

ABOUT HEIMY LEE LIBU MOLINA
Heimy Lee Libu Molina completed her engineering (honours) with

a first-class honours award and the university medal, majoring in civil engineering at Western Sydney University in 2022. She is a consistent dean's merit lister and awardee of the Vice Chancellor's Excellence Award, Women in STEM Education Champion and Emerging Designer of the Year. She is currently a graduate engineer at Gamuda in Australia, working on the Sydney Metro West – Western Tunnelling Package project. Heimy is currently a committee member for Young Engineers Australia (Sydney Division) and Women in Nuclear (Australia Division) and has been featured in talks (in schools and universities) seminars, podcasts, articles and panels, highlighting her impactful contributions to the industry. Aside from this, Heimy is a 7News Young Achiever Awards 2023 finalist and People's Choice awardee and a nominee for Engineers Australia's Emerging Professional Engineer of the Year.

Operating in the mentoring, training and advisory industry myself, it's proven that only 10% of people in the world will abide by this upcoming principle. Because fundamentally, only a minority desire to cultivate a mindset and skill set that is advanced and progressive to make their vision come into fruition, teamed with having skin in the game. Majority also do not stay in the investment game, but those that do, have to win. The universe will always reward investors. Malik Khan was my first client when I started The Construction Coach back in 2019, and I have to take the opportunity to share a story. On the eve of my first networking event in 2020, Malik's car was broken into, the criminals taking with them the suit he bought for the evening. Most people in their early twenties wouldn't show up or would simply wear what's available. Not Malik, who went out, got a new suit and showed up with full positivity, went on to meet Ron Malhotra that evening, and the rest became history. Delve deeply into what Malik's secret is that constructed such an investor's mindset at every opportunity, even when circumstances stated otherwise.

12

KEY TO GREATNESS

BY MALIK KHAN

WHAT IS ONE THING YOU WOULD TELL A PERSON?

Fear not what would happen if you invest in yourself, but what will happen if you don't.

WHY?

In the world of construction, the ultimate secret that holds the key to unlocking our true greatness and discovering more of our potential is through investing in ourselves and not indulging in self-doubts that arise when you're presented with the opportunity to do so. Just like a master architect meticulously constructs a magnificent building, we have within us the ability to construct an extraordinary life filled with success, fulfilment and happiness when we first give more to ourselves, instead of waiting for others to do it for us.

Reflecting on my journey from belonging to a family of six with financial constraints, to being an international student in a whole new country and to the person I have become now and to the person I will be in the future, I have not only been passionate about self-development but also follow it through with the drive to make the change within myself. It was through my upbringing where my parents are my superheroes in my life who have faced plentiful obstacles and are firm believers of investing in personal development and not being a product of their circumstances. Whenever I have faced challenges, I have always looked back onto my dad's personal life who has never given into any uncertainties and always held his head high in the face of any adversity life has thrown his way and held himself accountable for every action he has taken in his lifetime. It's him that has brought this principle to life for me and given me the courage to invest first, receive later. Can you do the same?

When I first entered the industry back in 2011, I decided to become a civil engineer going through a bachelor's degree in India. I had been unsure how I would perform, and little did I know if I would ever become competent or successful within my career or if this was the best career choice for someone who was eighteen years old back then. I assumed the notion that if I were to become an engineer, I would be successful through my technical skills or what I had learned during my undergraduate. However, in the midst of all the thoughts and self-doubts, I have always had the fear of what am I going to achieve in my future, or will I ever be competent? Or recognised? Fast-forward four years towards the end of my bachelor's, I realised that all this technical education didn't suffice in the face of my dreams or provide me with real answers to my vision, how to get there and also who am I as a person? All the peers around me had to say was to undertake a postgraduate degree, but I knew something wasn't adding up …

Instead, I took a massive chance and invested in myself via a one-way ticket to Australia, arriving in July 2016. I thought if I continue my higher education, I will also expand my life education and experiences at the same time. It was a massive risk for me at the time, and I can't say those first few years were easy. During my master's degree, I had failed in multiple units, paid substantial international student fees, worked multiple odd jobs just to attain the master's degree with the assumption that it will help me to land a professional job upon completion. At the time, it was a challenge, but because I invested in myself, it shaped my character, my fortitude and heightened my risk appetite and speed in my decisions, because I was vehemently against accepting a standard, struggling life here. I had to make a *return* on my investment for myself.

THE POWER OF SELF-INVESTMENT

Despite the significant financial, emotional and mental investment I'd made in coming to Australia, I still wasn't satisfied with the level of my results. Especially as I thought, with my varied experiences to date, I'd be able to enter the job market in Australia with relative ease, but that too didn't prove to be the case. So, my investment in self continued, through networking events, books, seminars, podcasts, coffee meetings. For an international student, I'd even invested in a new suit (which for someone like me back then, was a big thing). Every investment I have made towards knowledge has paid and is still paying the dividends in my personal and professional life. Because I never sought to make moves based on the perception of what I am 'losing' or 'giving away now', but only in terms of what I can gain. It's this fundamental paradigm shift that saw me energetically see that I can only continue to gain and experience more achievements when I give first. So, I continued to seek more ways to invest in myself – energetically, financially, mentally and not rely on what majority of society does – their degree.

YOUR TIME: THE MOST VALUABLE ASSET

As we have heard numerous times, 'Time is the most precious resource we possess.' I remember a version of myself where I used to say, 'I do not have enough time to invest into myself or do anything outside my comfort zone.' However, my excuses were not yielding results and I was not closer to my vision, which made me realise that every individual on this planet has twenty-four hours in a day and the determining factor is how you utilise it, which is the determining factor of your journey to growth. Choosing to spend my time on self-investment was/is challenging as I had to sacrifice hangouts with friends, parties or weekend outings, since if I want to become unbreakable as an individual it could not be attained without sacrifice. It was quite distinct by this time that greatness is not achieved through complacency or stagnation but through the commitment in pursuit of knowledge, taking consistent actions, being disciplined, making the commitment to learn, reflecting on your own journey and growing in the process.

All the time I have sacrificed, from sleeping for only four to five hours a day or working for over fourteen hours a day, investing at least an hour to learn new things and challenge my own beliefs, has made me who I am currently and helped me overcome my fears of failure, develop courage, define my vision and not falter in the face of adversity which will undoubtedly pay off in the long run. If you already think that your plate is full, then the results you experience are all that you will get to experience. So, you can decide if you would like to uphold the narrative of 'I don't have time' or choose one that better serves you.

MENTORSHIP

Mentoring is a critical path to one's journey of self-development. It is never about instant gratification or having immediate tangible results or what you want to hear. It is about overcoming the fears, constantly challenging yourself to let go of your own ignorance, being open to learning and courageous enough to take the actions and holding ourselves accountable for our mistakes. Mentoring is the knockout ring where we should be knocked out during the practise, rather than bleeding in war. The power of mentorship should not be underestimated in the construction industry, and is one that I closely embrace. I remember the early days of my career and the need for seeking guidance from mentors who have excelled within the industry before us.

I remember being sceptical on how mentoring is going to provide me the results that I seek. Are my mentors going to show me the life hacks or any tricks? The answer is no. If anything, mentorship is ensuring we are not taking the shortcuts. I have been extremely grateful for my parents' upbringing who've taught me the importance of investing in myself; I have had an amazing opportunity to learn from my dad who was my first mentor and role model, followed by Elinor Moshe who became my mentor, and through her, I had an opportunity to network and meet Ron Malhotra and Caroline Vass who have shown me the power of self-investment and the raw potential I had which was ready to be tapped into, and their belief in my potential which I had not been aware of at that time. And safe to say all my mentors have knocked me down to ensure I am accountable for my actions. It was only possible through dedication of time, resources and effort with a desire to learn and grow.

While writing this chapter, from being a construction professional, I have not only started a consulting business of my own but am also in the process of setting up a traditional construction business in the midst of challenging times within the construction industry. This would have not been possible if I had purely relied on technical skills or my academics. I have recognised the importance of holding myself accountable, investing in knowledge, personal growth, networking and wellbeing, that has set myself on a path of continuous improvement.

Remember that each investment we make towards self-**development** is an investment towards a brighter future filled with new opportunities and achievements and be ready to seize the opportunity to become an influential force within this ever-evolving field of construction.

ABOUT MALIK KHAN

Malik Khan is passionate about empowering young graduates and undergraduates in the pursuit of their career in their respective fields. He has a Bachelor's in Civil Engineering (India) and Master's of Construction and Infrastructure Management (Swinburne University, Australia). With a built understanding of the engineering, manufacturing and construction industries in India and Australia, his experiences currently see him working as a professional construction consultant for builders and developers. This chapter principle has assisted Malik Khan in managing a construction business with a vision to bring the construction industry back to its glory and contribute to the safety, health, environmental and effectiveness of society.

Your monkey mind tells you to run! Take it easy, you don't need more challenges in your life ... Do you think the upper echelon of any game have a disposition of running away from the fire or towards the fire? Now, no-one is telling you to get burnt, but how much heat can you handle? The more complexity you can go through, for long periods of time, will directly reflect your success. Yet, no-one sits down with you to give you a winning road map to make it to the other side. How important of a skill set this is, how underdeveloped it also is. Dr Priyadarshini Das has you covered with one of the industry's best-kept secrets

...

13

EMBRACING COMPLEXITY

BY DR PRIYADARSHINI DAS

WHAT IS ONE THING YOU WOULD TELL A PERSON?

Embrace complexity.

WHY?

One key lesson from my industry journey is the importance of embracing complexity. While it's tempting to wish for prior knowledge of this principle, its essence lies in iterative and continuous learning – something that inherently cannot be known prematurely. However, with this book in your hands, you've already seized a valuable opportunity. There are several steps to embracing something – the first is always a buy-in; you must realise that there's value in embracing it.

BUY-IN: THE TREASURE WITHIN COMPLEXITY

Complexity signifies numerous parts and their intricate connections that challenge our conventional comprehension and predictability. It's a maze where every turn can lead to a dead end or a hidden treasure. It's tempting, when faced with intricacies, to wash our hands of it – to label something as 'complicated' and push it to someone else's desk (outsource it). But herein lies a missed opportunity. True complexity is not a mere complication but a situation that no-one has experimented with yet. It's depth, richness and potential. It's the gold mine of innovation. When teams collaborate, brainstorm and dive deep into these complexities, they don't just find solutions – they establish new norms. This is the realm where the status quo is challenged and growth is achieved. Once you have bought into it, the next step would be acceptance of it.

ACCEPT THAT MOST PROBLEMS DON'T HAVE LINEAR SOLUTIONS - BE COMFORTABLE WITH TRADE-OFFS

In the vast and multifaceted field of construction, newcomers and veterans alike face a common realisation: straight lines rarely lead directly to successful solutions. In a realm where physical elements intersect with theoretical plans, where weather can change a day's course, linearity is a luxury. This might initially seem intimidating, but the vast number of variables makes the industry a playground for problem-solvers. To successfully navigate this landscape, it's vital to understand the concept of trade-offs.

Consider a function, for instance:

Function = Benefit / (Cost + Harm)

This equation may appear simple, but it encapsulates an essential idea. It's not solely about chasing benefits; it's about comprehending the balance between rewards, costs and potential pitfalls. To thrive in construction, one must be comfortable with this delicate balance. Once you have accepted complexity, it is important to understand the impact of complexity.

THERE WILL ALWAYS BE A COMPLEX WEB OF CHOICES, AND EVERY CHOICE HAS RIPPLE EFFECTS

Construction is all about decisions. Decisions that have seemingly small immediate impacts can lead to significant, far-reaching consequences. Consider the placement of a single window. This choice affects light, aesthetics, energy efficiency, cost and even the behaviour of the building's occupants. Each choice in construction is like throwing a stone into a pond, creating ripples that touch every facet of the project. The key is not to be paralysed by this. Instead, understand and anticipate these ripples. Recognise that a shift in materials or a change in design doesn't just impact the immediate area; it can reshape the entire outcome of a project. And what do you do when you have a complex web of choice, you guesstimate!

GUESSTIMATE: BRIDGING THEORY AND REALITY

Within the vast spectrum of construction decisions, not every answer comes packaged in neat, quantifiable boxes. That's where the art of 'guesstimating' becomes invaluable. Roles such as business analyst or data scientist might seem distant from the rough-and-tumble of a construction site. Still, these professionals often hold the project's backbone. Using their informed guesstimates, they bridge the gap between theoretical planning and on-ground realities. However, it's essential to note the evolution that professionals should aim for transitioning from accuracy to precision. Starting with an educated guess (percentage accuracy) and, through iterations, refining this guess to be closer to the desired outcome (precision). This journey involves prototyping and feedback – trial and error, learning and adapting.

EXPERIMENTING AND FEEDBACK ARE NON-NEGOTIABLES

While construction is grounded in the tangible – concrete, steel, wood – it's also about the intangible. It's about ideas, innovations and experiments. No blueprint, however detailed, can anticipate every challenge or opportunity on a construction site. This is where the courage to experiment comes into play. Whether testing a new material or implementing a novel construction technique, innovation is the bedrock of progress. But experimentation isn't reckless abandon; it's a measured approach that demands resources. For complex challenges, these resources – time, money, expertise – are the tickets to solutions. Every experiment is a question posed, and feedback provides the answer. Embracing complexity, thus, is more than just a mindset. It's a strategy. Complexity is not a hindrance but a call to action, a beckoning to think beyond the obvious, to embrace challenges and to uncover the myriad possibilities they present. Whether you are a seasoned professional or a novice stepping into the construction arena, the secret to success lies in understanding, accepting and leveraging this complexity.

A COMPLEXITY CANVAS: NAVIGATING COMPLEXITY

Our inherent aversion to complexity is deeply rooted in our

cognitive disposition. Fear of the unknown and layered problems that complexity triggers daunt the human mind. Adding to it, embracing complexity is a slow brew, which makes us reluctant to pursue it. Contrastingly, leaders who lean into complexity often exhibit a higher tolerance for ambiguity and understand that within the intricate web of complexity lie unexplored opportunities and unconventional solutions that can drive innovation and long-term growth. As professionals grapple with understanding and embracing complexity, it becomes vital to possess a structured framework to untangle this web and strategise effectively. Enter the 'Complexity Canvas'. Inspired by Alexander Osterwalder's business model canvas, the Complexity Canvas is a visual and conceptual framework designed around nine pivotal elements that can guide professionals, irrespective of their domain or level, to have the strategic courage essential for embracing complexity. A canvas is typically a visual tool designed to help teams or individuals think through a complex topic in a structured way, so this complexity canvas has been designed with clarity and usability in mind.

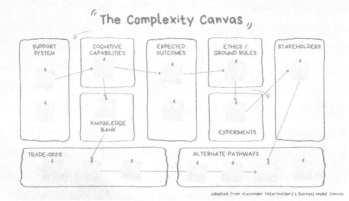

Image by Dr Priyadarshi Das

ELEMENT 1: SUPPORT SYSTEM

Your support system is the bedrock upon which you build. They provide guidance, perspective and often a safety net.

- **Core team:** These people know you intimately – your family, spouse or close colleagues with shared experiences. They offer a foundation of trust and mutual understanding.
- **Mentors:** Teachers, bosses or senior colleagues who guide based on their experience and insights.
- **Influencers:** The industry leaders you admire and follow, perhaps on platforms like LinkedIn. Their journeys showcase what's possible and set a benchmark for success.

ELEMENT 2: COGNITIVE CAPABILITIES

These are the mental tools you bring to the table. Your inherent abilities and skills, like processing power, negotiation techniques and communication, form the gears of your operational mechanism.

ELEMENT 3: KNOWLEDGE BANK

Knowledge isn't static; it's dynamic. As the saying goes, 'knowledge is power', and in a rapidly evolving world, continuously updating and expanding your knowledge reservoir becomes paramount.

ELEMENT 4: EXPECTED OUTCOMES

Define what you seek. By clarifying expectations, you set a direction for your journey. If life were a project, some of the expected outcomes could be as follows:

- **Desired position attributes:** Maybe a role that aligns with your strengths.
- **Geographic aspirations:** Perhaps a job that lets you globe-trot.
- **Work-life integration:** A position that offers you the time and flexibility for personal pursuits.
- **Organisational culture:** A preference for workplaces that have flat hierarchies, ensuring open communication and minimal bureaucracy.

ELEMENT 5: ETHICS/GROUND RULES

Your moral compass. By establishing ethical parameters, you ensure that your professional journey remains aligned with your core values.

ELEMENT 6: TRIAL RUNS/EXPERIMENTS

Through work breakdown structures and pilot experiments – prototyping – you iterate, refine and move closer to the optimal solution, ensuring minimal missteps.

ELEMENT 7: STAKEHOLDERS

By understanding and adeptly managing stakeholders, you not only anticipate varied perspectives and needs but also foster a supportive environment to navigate through the intricate pathways of complexity. Engage stakeholders in ideation and development stages, leveraging their insights to craft more inclusive and robust solutions.

ELEMENT 8: TRADE-OFFS

Every decision comes with its benefits and costs. Recognising and understanding these trade-offs means making informed choices. This element should list potential trade-offs to consider, such as:

- Time vs. Quality.
- Cost vs. Sustainability.
- Immediate gains vs. Long-term benefits.
- Individual success vs. Team growth.

ELEMENT 9: ALTERNATE PATHWAYS

Rarely is there a single road to success. By identifying multiple pathways, you remain adaptable and open to possibilities. This section should list potential alternatives or strategies to reach your goals, for example:

- Traditional vs. Modern approaches.
- Direct vs. Indirect pathways.
- Quick wins vs. Slow and steady progression.
- Self-driven learning vs. Structured formal education.

As professionals advancing in your careers, the Complexity Canvas can be a trusted ally, continually helping you recalibrate and navigate the interrelationships with clarity, confidence and purpose. By populating this canvas, you not only map out the current interrelationships but also chart a course for their desired future, making complexity your ally, not an adversary.

ABOUT DR PRIYADARSHINI DAS

Priya is a postdoctoral research fellow in the department of civil engineering at Monash University, working on several building 4.0 CRC projects that explore the platform ecosystem business model in construction. With a doctorate from Western Sydney University, her interests lie in Industry 4.0 applications within construction. Before commencing her doctoral research, Priya worked for Larsen and Toubro Construction for over half a decade in the planning, monitoring and control systems of transportation infrastructure projects such as highways, runways and elevated corridors. She also had a short stint with the US-based technology-driven construction startup Katerra, where she was part of the scrum team that developed Katerra's construction project management software suite, Apollo. Priya has a fervour for content creation, from contributing to esteemed academic journals to curating engaging LinkedIn pages.

You have an empirically tough call to make. Who do you turn to? If, in your response, the first person that you mentioned wasn't your own inner guidance system, you're misleading yourself. There is a massive difference in listening to your monkey mind versus your intuition. Everything you've always wanted to know is available to you, right now. Yet, you've locked it away, choosing to play the game via the opinions and scraps provided by others. Brenda Kiptugen offers you a glimpse into how to turn the mirror back onto yourself, to access more wisdom than what any other person even, can have to offer you.

Let's venture within ...

14

HARNESSING INTUITION FOR INNOVATION AND INSIGHT

BY BRENDA KIPTUGEN

WHAT IS ONE THING YOU WOULD TELL A PERSON?

Intuition is your guiding light in the depths of the unknown – dare to pursue it in making great decisions.

WHY?

Back in the spring of 2018, I found myself confined to my bed for three days, engrossed in TED Talks, desperately seeking answers. How could I possibly muster the courage to inform my parents that I was once again abandoning a degree I had passionately begged them to allow me to pursue? It had happened twice before, and I felt my world unravelling. I had always used academia as validation of my self-worth, so admitting that I wouldn't become an engineer was a devastating blow. My version of doomsday, or as I now affectionately call it, 'The Pivot', had come calling, and the only voice that could reassure me I was on the right path was that quiet, unwavering inner intuition. When the opportunity arose to share my not-so-secret secret about how I contribute to the construction industry, I knew this was it. Fundamentally, I had the light-bulb moment of my life – I must listen to myself.

Trusting my intuition has opened numerous doors, guiding me through career choices and helping me identify my unique offering to the industry. With an open heart and a childlike curiosity to discover what more I can do to serve my community, I've come to appreciate that intuition, often overlooked in construction, holds the potential to break the mould of the industry in profound ways, allowing room for more individuality and creative expression.

In the world of construction, there's a unique magic in being a creator. We have the privilege to kickstart a project from its very foundations and watch it blossom into a magnificent edifice or a critical piece of infrastructure. What makes this process truly remarkable is the journey itself – the questions asked, the constant quest for answers and the realisation that, more often than not, we operate in an environment where clear information is scarce. We're often required to make decisions with courage and patience when faced with ambiguity. The ability to harness intuition isn't just about our day-to-day tasks; it extends to shaping our careers and interactions with others.

THE PSYCHOLOGY OF INTUITION

Our journey into the realm of intuition delves deep into the very psychology that guides our decision-making. Many are quick to dismiss it as unreliable, vague or irrational. It's crucial, however, to ask the question – why does intuition face this scepticism?

To embark on a journey of self-discovery and develop a strong connection with our intuition, it begins with acknowledging our human design. Part of this human experience is making mistakes. Yet, society has, at times, cultivated an environment where errors are met with guilt and shame. These negative emotions can surround our wrong decisions, making it difficult to accept and learn from them. 'If you put shame in a Petri dish, it needs three things to grow exponentially: secrecy, silence and judgement. If you put the same amount of shame in a Petri dish and douse it with empathy, it can survive,' says Dr Brené Brown.

The connection between 'gut-feel receptors' and our intuition is an intriguing facet of human biology and psychology. While traditionally, intuition has been associated with processes in the brain, emerging research points to the presence of an extensive network of neurons, often referred to as the 'second brain', residing in the human gut. This network, known as the enteric nervous system, contains a multitude of receptors and sensory neurons that communicate with the brain. The gut-brain axis, a bidirectional communication system, facilitates the transmission of information from the gut to the brain, playing a crucial role in our intuitive processes. This intricate network suggests that the 'gut feeling' we often experience is not merely a metaphorical expression; it is rooted in the physiological connections that allow the gut to send signals to the brain, influencing our decision-making, emotional responses and intuitive insights. Understanding this connection provides a compelling framework for exploring the role of gut instincts in decision-making and highlights the complex interplay between our physical and mental states. When was the last time you listened to your gut to make a decision?

In my personal experience, growing up in an ethnic family, the weight of familial and cultural expectations added an extra layer to this challenge. It was a continuous battle to overcome the guilt and shame stemming from making the wrong decision. However, I gradually transformed this perspective. I came to view a wrong decision not as a failure but as a valuable learning opportunity. It's through these missteps that we gain insights, gather wisdom and refine our intuitive abilities.

Cultivating a stronger bond with our intuition demands a mindful practice of keenly observing the contextual information at our disposal. In any given scenario, the quantity and quality of available information significantly influences the dynamic interplay between intuition and intellect. When we encounter situations where information is scarce, intuition emerges as the guiding force, stepping into the forefront of our decision-making processes.

'Visionary decision-making happens at the intersection of intuition and logic.' – Paul O'Brien, author of
Great Decisions, Perfect Timing

It becomes the compass guiding us when conventional reasoning falls short. Conversely, when we have a wealth of data and facts at our disposal, our intellect tends to dominate our decision-making process. Striking a balance between these two forces is key to greater innovation and insight personally and professionally.

Yet, achieving this equilibrium is not a solitary pursuit; it's about fostering an internal environment where both our cognitive reasoning and emotional sensibilities coexist and are valued. It is within this realm of internal harmony that intuition thrives. Here, the conscious alignment of rational analysis with emotional insight forms the foundation for more profound intuitive connections so that you can fundamentally make more progressive decisions for your personal and collective betterment.

By acknowledging our inherent human fallibility, comprehending the societal conditioning that often surrounds us and actively nurturing the coexistence of our thoughts and emotions, we pave the way for a richer and more profound connection with our intuition. In this transformative process, intuition evolves from an enigmatic force into a reliable ally within the construction industry. This ally empowers us to gracefully navigate the intricate landscapes of our projects, making confident decisions even amidst the complexities and sensory overload of the modern construction world.

PRACTICAL APPLICATIONS OF INTUITION

Practically, intuition plays a pivotal role in risk assessments and mitigation. Safety is paramount in our projects, and sometimes, even when the numbers align, a gut feeling signals something isn't right. Honest conversations that allow concerns to be voiced are crucial in such situations. In the complex world of construction, where coordination involves resources, time lines and budgets, intuition becomes an invaluable asset for project managers. It aids in anticipating delays, foreseeing bottlenecks and making agile adjustments to keep projects on course. If you feel something isn't right, it probably isn't.

Making career moves often involves pivotal decisions where intuition plays a crucial role. It's those moments when you feel an inner tug, wanting to say yes when you've initially said no, or vice versa. These intuitive prompts can be a compass guiding you towards the right path. Sometimes, our logical analysis might lead us in one direction, while our gut feelings pull us in another. Embracing your intuition in these instances is akin to trusting your inner wisdom, which is often rooted in accumulated experiences and emotional intelligence. Saying yes when your intuition urges you can lead to unexpected opportunities and personal growth. Conversely, heeding a strong inner 'no' can help you avoid choices that might not align with your authentic self. In navigating the intricate landscape of career decisions, tuning into your intuitive signals can lead to more authentic and fulfilling professional journeys.

Embracing intuition grounds us and enables creative exploration that goes beyond the limits of our current understanding as an industry. We know that the demands of the construction world are ever-changing, so new solutions are required to respond to new inquiries. Intuition empowers individuals to push the boundaries of logic, knowing that their intuitive insight provides the boldness to pursue a vision that may not be visible to anyone else.

Recognising where intuition has led to successful decisions and using that evidence to trust your gut is a missed opportunity.

Intuition isn't a mere abstract concept; it's a key to achieving a harmonious balance between your mind and heart, the foundation of operating in flow. I urge you to explore how and why intuition should be an integral part of construction operations, enriching decision-making processes and ultimately benefiting not only the industry but society as a whole.

Here's a little exercise I've found handy when I want to connect with my sixth sense while making decisions. I keep it simple by asking myself a straightforward yes-or-no question and pay close attention to the immediate response from my heart space. If it feels like a warm expansion, that's a clear yes. But if it's like an internal tug or retraction back into my body, that's a solid no. I know it might sound a bit cheesy or like something out of a mystical realm, but give it a go before you judge! The truth is, the more you practise this mind-heart connection, the closer you get to making it a natural part of your self-awareness and decision-making process. It's like training a muscle, and every day you work on it, you're one step closer to having a reliable asset in your decision-making sphere.

ABOUT BRENDA KIPTUGEN

Brenda Kiptugen is an accomplished professional with a proven track record of delivering successful projects in the realms of commercial construction and mining infrastructure. With a wealth of experience garnered from collaborating across several Fortune 500 companies, Brenda has honed her expertise in cost estimation, project management and contract administration. Her exceptional communication skills and unwavering dedication to achieving results have made her a trusted asset in the industry.

Beyond her professional achievements, Brenda is a passionate advocate for diversity and inclusion, actively engaging in community initiatives and volunteering with organisations like NAWIC and AIB. Her commitment to continuous learning and her unique perspective on the integration of intuition in construction decision-making make Brenda an influential voice in the field. Her chapter explores the profound ways in which intuition can transform the industry and foster creative thinking. Brenda's invaluable contributions have positioned her as a true leader and change-maker in the construction world.

It may seem inconsequential when you park your desires and dreams on a daily basis. Then, the days turn into weeks, weeks to months, months to years, years to decades, decades to your funeral, and all this time, you've placated and suppressed that inner voice begging you to make a move, in the smallest of ways, for yourself. It's likely you're hyper-wired to feel guilt and shame for doing something for yourself, and that belief is fundamentally working against you. This young gun, in such a short time from starting anew in a foreign country, has been able to apply his winning principle to achieve what would take the majority decades. Sarbjeet Singh demonstrates the power of this possibility when you only have to do this one thing and watch how your dreams and desires unfold …

15

THE 1% MINDSET

BY SARBJEET SINGH

WHAT IS ONE THING YOU WOULD TELL A PERSON?

Do something extra every single day.

WHY?

It could be the thing that defines who you are as a person and separates you from others. This 'something extra' could be something as simple as reading ten pages of a book or maybe listening to a TED Talk. Trust me, this extra work that you will put in towards yourself will get compounded, and within one to two years, you will get to see the results and realise the positive impact this has created in your life and career. One thing we need to clarify here is that the result from the 'extra work' would only be positive if you do something that has the power to bring a small positive change in you on a day-to-day basis. This is how I am making sure that I am at least 1% better every day. Now, how do I do that? Let's know a bit about my story and how I started to get the answer.

I came to Australia in 2020, and everything that I have done so far has been accomplished within three years of moving. I was born in a small town in India and my family runs a small business. I am the only one in my family who has ever gotten a university degree. So, where did it all come from? Well, I kept myself open to learning new things and becoming better day by day until I got the results I wanted. If someone has already achieved something and you would like to do something similar, talking to that person and listening to their journey, you know the answers to the problems that they faced on their way. That's a key strategy I used to constantly expand myself when most people will come to a new country only to not speak to anyone, and how I also avoided missing opportunities for daily betterment. Successful people are always willing to share their journey. To be successful in anything you do, it is really important to master the art of compound effect and knowing how to bring that into action. There's a common misconception that one or two actions will yield results, but I know that only by doing one extra thing daily for myself can I get results – and this requires immense patience too. The results from your work are never instant and you just have to keep on putting in the effort until you get what you want. The question to ask yourself is, are you willing to do it daily, with no pats on the backs and results in the short-term?

The year I started studying at university, everything went into lockdown because of the pandemic. Being new to the country where no-one even spoke my first language and having no friends made things really overwhelming. I was staying in the student accommodation and would just study. I joined a few community groups as a volunteer because I was told by one of my seniors at the university that building connections is important in the long run and volunteering would help me enhance my transferrable skills. Doing this for the whole year, I could see the results. I became more confident with my English, I became good at having conversations with people and connecting with them and I learnt how to lead – which I only get to experience because of my 1% daily determination.

At one of my coffee catch-ups, I was told, 'If you can't find an opportunity then create one.' So, in my second year of university (2021), I was confident enough to start a study group of my own. I created a study group where we would help the new international students transition to university life. This led me to another role at my university and I became a mentor for the English language students. My efforts with these initiatives were recognised and I was awarded with the 'Students Helping Students' award which is the highest-level leadership award at my university. I highlight this to you to reinforce that results do come with focused and strategic daily action. And this type of action isn't doing the bare minimum. Most students will consider their plates full just with their studies. My 1% attitude enabled me to see past that and not consider myself already limited and at capacity. So, ask yourself, why have you limited your capacity when 1% can change your whole year?

Only because I feared a certain feeling, I would deliberately put myself into that situation so that I could keep working towards making myself 1% better. I was invited to be an ambassador for an organisation called Study Geelong then later became ambassadors for Engineers Australia and Deakin University. Although these roles only involved volunteering, I never treated them as if they were unpaid. I remember that one of my friends asked me to focus on my paid work and studies and stop doing all this, however, I kept engaging myself in these roles as they were making me better. These volunteering roles worked like superannuation where you keep on putting in the money (you keep on working) and you get the return on your retirement (when you get to use the learnt skills in real world). It was challenging for me to keep working on these roles as I am an international student, however, I would question myself, when was the last time I was given the opportunity to speak to hundreds of people? When was the last time I led a team of twenty people for an initiative? When was the last time I launched an ad campaign? Working on these roles made me do all this and more. I keep telling myself that at least I am getting the exposure to some of the best situations that may come across again when I shift to the corporate industry. Again, it's the 1% mentality to not cancel out opportunity.

I was finally able to see the effects of the compounding. I was able to secure a role with the local council as an intern and was later promoted to the position of undergraduate engineer. I was then promoted again to a full-time engineering position at the end of my third year at university and for the first ever time, the council decided to make that role part-time to suit my preferences. I was then able to take part in the university election and be elected to the role of campus coordinator where I would lead a team of eight campus representatives and foresee the activities of thirty-five university clubs. I then started a university club myself, and as a president of that club, I was able to make it one of the biggest clubs of my university. This wouldn't have been possible if I didn't first seek to have conversations years ago. No destination is arrived to by sheer chance.

I have seen the effects of compounding on a firsthand basis. From a shy personality whose speech would fumble and legs would shake when standing in front of a crowd to being MC for some of the biggest events, leading teams, being a guest speaker for events, hosting welfare initiatives and addressing important issues such as food insecurity and student housing, I have changed myself – not overnight, not even in a month, but over years. It all started with one step at a time. Now I have been awarded the Geelong Youth Award 2023 for my contribution to the local community and have been named as the finalist for the International Student of the Year Award.

Although I have not yet reached where I want to go, I can give you the magic formula for being successful in whatever you do. The formula is not good looks, it's not being rich, it's not IQ and it's not physical health. The formula is the 'compound effect'. It's about your passion combined with perseverance for a very long-term goal. So, start getting comfortable with being uncomfortable and as said by Henry David Thoreau, 'Success usually comes to those who are too busy to be looking for it.' Get busy and start working towards yourself and making sure you are at least 1% better every day.

ABOUT SARBJEET SINGH

Sarbjeet, a final-year Bachelor of Civil Engineering student, exemplifies dedication to academics and community service. He currently works as a stormwater engineer at the Geelong City Council while completing his thesis. Sarbjeet's impact extends beyond the classroom and workplace, as he serves as an ambassador for Study Geelong, Engineers Australia and Deakin University.

At Deakin University, he's an elected student council member and president of the Indian Club, fostering cultural inclusivity. Committed to community welfare, Sarbjeet addresses issues like student housing, flood affordability and LGBTIQ+ rights.

His remarkable contributions have earned him the Geelong Youth Award and recognition as the winner of Premier's International Student of the Year Award.

Sarbjeet's journey exemplifies the transformative power of education and leadership in creating a positive impact. In academia, profession and community advocacy, Sarbjeet's unwavering dedication shines bright, inspiring others to follow his lead.

What are you really ready for? Have you put yourself in a precarious situation that if your world were to unexpectedly flip on you, would you sink or swim? If a major crisis found its way to you, what would happen? Au contraire – a major opportunity looms on the horizon, are you in a position to make a move? Think about the myriad of situations that may meet you, tomorrow, and consider what position you have put yourself in to respond to it. Jenny Tseng remains ready. She's not one that likes to leave things to chance – not one for surprises. She knows that you can't be in the battlefield without the right strategy in arms. So, she's going to give you a secret code …

16

The Preparedness Code

BY JENNY TSENG

What is one thing you would tell a person?

Knowing is not doing, and doing without direction is risky. For whatever we cannot control in life, we absolutely shall prepare for what's possible to come.

Why?

The Principle of Preparedness

Preparedness is a reflection on the series of encounters faced each day and how effectively we manage situations and decision-making in life. What's more, the direction of these preparations is something that we must master to achieve success in our personal endeavours.

The construction industry is a massive ecosystem and extremely volatile. We are living it every day, serving our time in an infinite loop to deliver projects after projects, design and innovate, while expected to advance our career pathway with a growth mindset.

Change is constant, and yet, so many people are waiting for things to happen. They think they can endure and adapt to changes effortlessly, only to be shocked that the next project or job is never better. Most individuals are not prepared to navigate through different situations and engage in ways to maximise their personal potential.

Throughout my career, I have heard numerous references to the two quotes, 'Opportunities are for those that are prepared,' and, 'Successes are for those that seized the moment,' and most of us still feel a lack of clarity and loss of direction. Many industry reports have identified the market trends, with business books putting further emphasis on the continuum of personal skills development. But the truth is, I haven't yet come across a source that covers the importance of preparedness with sufficient depth and relevance to the construction industry. Why should we prepare and what are we preparing for? And how can you recognise the opportunities to capture and seize them with ease? Enter, the preparedness code.

WHY DOES PREPAREDNESS MATTER?

Preparedness means to be in a consistent state of readiness and already in 'ing' mode, actioning the thoughts in mind that align with your values. The main benefit of preparedness is knowing that you'll be fully equipped and organised, taken proactive measures and acquired the necessary knowledge or resources to effectively deal with a specific situation or any set of circumstances.

As individuals, we cannot control the uncontrollable in the construction industry, which is the upturn and downturn of our economy. Don't we all wish to have the psychic power to predict the future and know what to do? The preparedness code enables us to anticipate the causes and manage the impact.

The upturn refers to the thriving periods advantageous to everyone. Setting ambitious yet attainable goals and cultivating new relationships are the best preparations to position yourself with opportunities that align with your aspirations. When the government announced its ten-year infrastructure pipeline, I recognised the considerable job prospects it held for progressing my career. Enhancing transport project experiences and joining industry communities not only equipped me to explore diverse career paths, but also expanded my professional network.

The downturn refers to the periods of instability and insecurity when we switch on survival mode. Upskilling, building resilience and growing personal strength are the main preparations at this time. When I was demobilised from a project after the Global Financial Crisis, I invested time into registering as an architect and managed to overcome the fear of uncertainty. Having ultimately left the company, I emerged with a greater resilience in the face of setbacks and increased competence to seek new pathways. Above all, I learned how to persevere when circumstance takes an unfavourable turn.

So, there are three keys I hold dear to my heart when preparing for these situations.

THE THREE KEYS OF THE PREPAREDNESS CODE

Key 1: Turn on the Change Switch

Do you always know where you are heading in your career? If you do, then I am envious and keen to know your secrets too. But for the majority, we often feel stuck and fall into the trap of yearly planning cycle without really changing the ways of moving forward.

After my first decade practising as an architect, I decided to diversify away from the design space. I still love architecture; however, it is the most vulnerable profession affected by any changes. Getting a promotion may be easier during good times, but it is still extremely competitive. Working in a major corporation seems beneficial during a downturn, you are likely to be dismissed when projects are placed on hold and costs are cut. Therefore, I refuse to leave my future to chances and determine to be my own champion of change.

The imperative step of owning change begins with taking the responsibility of *knowing your needs*. Conducting a simple *hierarchy of needs self-assessment* (Figure 1) is essential. First, it shows the needs deficiencies within your current situation like my employment prospects no longer suffice in meeting my basic safety requirements for emotional and financial security. Second, it highlights the personal impact you must address such as rediscovering my own strength and regain recognition to boost my self-esteem. Third, it assists with your action plan prioritisation; in my case, making the conscious decision to switch runway into the digital domain was my top priority.

Figure 1: Hierarchy of needs assessment
Source: Created by Jenny Tseng based on Mcleod, 2023

Needs Deficiency	Personal Impact	Action Plan
Self-actualisation desire to become the most that one can be	1. Finance security 2. Emotional security 3. Low self-esteem 4. Unknown strength 5. Lack of recognition 6. Missing career opportunities	1. Change career pathway 2. Find new job opportunities 3. Learn new skills 4. Mentoring/ Coaching programs 5. Event speaking
Esteem respect, self-esteem, status, recognition, strength, freedom		
Love and belonging friendship, intimacy, family, sense of connection		
Safety needs personal security, employment, resources, health, property		
Physiological needs air, water, food, shelter, sleep, clothing, reproduction		

This process must be iterative when the situation changes to be most effective, so establish a regular cadence that works for you. I redo my own assessment quarterly to keep my hierarchy relevant. Importantly, one should not satisfy all levels of needs simultaneously prior to initiating other change.

Key 2: Design Your Lego Set

The essence of designing your Lego set is the ability to collect a variety of blocks in colours, shapes and sizes to transform your current role into what you want to become along your career pathway (Figure 2). The blocks symbolise transferrable skills that we require to build capability for transformation. If you don't hold the right pieces, what Lego do you expect to build for yourself?

Figure 2: Lego set transformation
Source: Jenny Tseng

No-one except yourself can set directions for the next *transition* and define what new blocks to *acquire*. I am lucky to state that what I am doing now is where I had envisaged myself ten years ago. My current role and position, although unconventional in their nature, embody the specialised field that I passionately sought to cultivate. But I had a road map to follow. The 'ABC' approach (Figure 3) is the technique I've developed for my transition journey using the present, expected and future structure.

Figure 3: Point ABC transitional approach
Source: Jenny Tseng

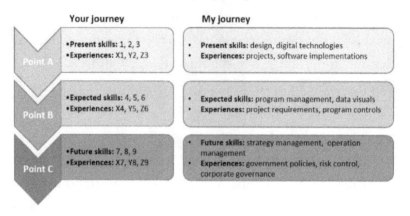

Point A is about the current state of play by evaluating your present skills and experiences as a baseline and what gaps to fill. Especially in downturn, you can navigate challenges with greater precision through the technical and transferable skills identified. Similar to how I can be certain of my software skills before transferring into a digital role.

Point B is the most critical transition that requires the most time, adjustments and perseverance in target setting. It is a definition phase when you make calculated moves to gain new capabilities. It took me four years to pick up additional expertise in data management and self-development like an MBA to arrive at point B in the advisory sector.

Point C is the future status, advancing towards the vision of where you aspire to be. My key advice is to make connections between all your knowledge, so they are relational and transferrable between each point. I was a project architect before a project manager, a digital specialist now heading towards digital consulting services as my point C.

Our career trajectory within the contemporary workplace

now follows an exponential rather than a linear path. As such, please don't waste time going down the traditional route and start asking, 'What is in your Lego box? Do you know what it looks like and where to find the missing blocks?'

Key 3: Dare to Let Go

We are all familiar with the age-old inquiry, 'Is your glass half-full or half-empty?' In today's context, I believe the more pertinent question would be, 'How fast are you filling up the glass and what should you tip out?' If you constantly feel overwhelmed by a never-ending to-do list, which I refer to as the 'glass overflowing mentality' (Figure 4), then it is time to let go.

Figure 4: Glass overflowing mentality
Source: Jenny Tseng

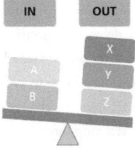

The concept of *dare to let go* centres around the mindset of relinquishing control rather than giving up and aims to alleviate our self-hindrance in any circumstances. When we are able to let go, we don't pretend to have all the capacity and capabilities; we empty our vessels to onboard new stock rather than hoarding; we understand how to ask the question rather than doing it all; we can mitigate burnout by managing our stress and emotions.

With the acceleration on the adoption of digital technologies and data-driven processes, the construction industry must now deal with a significant demand for information and faster *rate of change*. Letting go on the notion of 'if not me, then no-one will' while dealing with change is challenging but can still be achieved through *collaborative delegation*. By creating a committed cohort group to attain the goals with identical values and consistently engage the people through collaborative activities and communications.

A great lesson learned on my journey is acknowledging that no-one is capable of doing everything and anything all at once. We tend to become the doers and forget to delegate to the teams to allow us more capacity to pursue other goals. My reinvented Lewin's force field analysis model (Figure 5) can offer a methodology to better the delegation decision-making process. By identifying the driving force like 'knowledge share' and resisting force like 'communication efforts' to compare the reasons for not wanting to let go. In order for change to occur, your driving force must exceed the resisting force.

Figure 5: Force field analysis model for delegation

I always strive to improve my work-life balance and ensure that I have the support tools in place. So, ask yourself why your glass is overflowing. How self-aware are you on the driving and resisting forces and how ready are you to let go?

UNLOCKING THE CODE

I hope you have found the preparedness code to be motivating and an inspirational discovery. The main purpose is to activate your mind into taking action to be prepared. On some level, you may already be on this journey and are prepared to see great results. I know the three keys work for me and will continue to collect more in the future.

The best way to think of the keys is as guiding steps for change in the construction industry where you are prepared to:

- Take responsibilities to turn on your change switch.
- Know what Lego pieces to collect in transit.

- Dare to let go of the uncontrollable personal burden.

REFERENCES

- Lewin, K 1958, Group decision and social change, *Readings in social psychology*, pp. 197 – 211, New York, NY: Holt, Rinehart, and Winston.
- Mcleod S, 2023, Maslow's Hierarchy of Needs, *Simply Psychology*, viewed 28 July 2023, www.simplypsychology.org/maslow.html

ABOUT JENNY TSENG

Jenny is an accomplished technical director in digital advisory and digital delivery practice lead at Mott MacDonald, boasting an impressive career spanning over two decades. Her expertise encompasses digital leadership, asset management and data governance, making her a global contributor to various industries.

Jenny's impactful journey includes pivotal client-side roles with TfNSW, Sydney Metro and Victoria Suburban Rail Loop Authority. Her specialist knowledge has been instrumental in driving industry-wide digital transformation and laid the foundation for governments' digital vision and strategies.

Beyond her technical acumen, Jenny also holds leadership positions in professional communities like Women in BIM as a board director. Jenny's vision is to empower all individuals to embrace digital innovation in the construction industry for greater diversity and social outcomes.

As quickly as a flame roars, can it be extinguished.
Yet, sometimes, the embers are still there, but
they need air to survive and become a flame that
remains, illuminates. Instead of fuel to the fire, you,
or someone else, will come with an ice bucket. And
there it goes. Then eventually, you won't want to start
any fires, because you've already killed off the idea
before it even had the chance to breathe. This same
ideology permeates society – teachers tell you to stop
daydreaming, people telling you to get your head out
of the clouds. No, don't. We need more illumination.
Contrary to popular belief, the engineering sector
thrives off creativity, and Marie O'Looney will reveal
the secret of how imperative it is to provide fuel, not
water, to your ideas ...

17

DO NOT RELINQUISH YOUR IDEAS TOO SOON

BY MARIE O'LOONEY

WHAT IS ONE THING YOU WOULD TELL A PERSON?

Do not relinquish your ideas too soon.

WHY?

Some people's need to be 'right' is crippling creativity in the construction industry.

'Don't waste your time thinking about that' and 'that's not going to work', 'do it this way' or 'this is the quicker way' are some phrases you may hear when you newly share an idea. This may seem okay at first as you set out on your learning journey, as you respect others' perspectives, however, it has the potential to stop you from thinking, hinder vocalising your ideas, diminish your curiosity and in turn affect creativity.

Some of these people are industry leaders and feel the pressure of a 'have it all together' facade for credibility with employees and clients/customers, letting ego get in the way of brilliant ideas. Doing so prevents leadership awareness about unhealthy behaviour patterns and the underlying 'blocks' or factors driving them. These blocks are explained further below.

Engineers are problem-solvers and generally want to be the first to answer or be the smartest person in the room. The more knowledge acquired, the more tendency there is to think an improvement is needed on the ideas of others. Whilst the quality of the idea may go up 5%, the commitment to execute it may go down 50%, because it is no longer the idea of the originator. Some people can also find it difficult to explore others' ideas if it's different to their way of thinking or if it hasn't been done before and so these ideas will likely get squashed entirely. Consider how many brilliant ideas have lost steam simply because of this dynamic ...

There are other reasons why people give up on their ideas too soon:

- We mistake lessons for failure – we fear making mistakes and when we inevitably do, we see it as a failure. We can then see failure before it happens and self-sabotage which leads to lack of self-belief in ourselves and our ideas.
- We can lack discipline and find it too hard to embrace change.
- We can become too focused on climbing the ladder that we dismiss the journey of curiosity and growth along the way; the journey is often where the magic happens and makes the end goal sweeter.

John E Arnold, psychologist and engineer, in the 1950s offered a course titled 'Creative Engineering' at Stanford University. He noted that in everyday life people are not always as creative as they might be because of certain 'blocks' in how they think about problems, how they engage in the problem-solving process, and how they conceive their personal roles and capabilities.

He categorised these blocks into perceptual, cultural and emotional. They are all intertwined, but emotional blocks dominate, as he explains, 'They include all our fears, and most of the defence mechanisms that we build up in order to make our lives seemingly more tolerable.'

Further emotional blocks include fear of making a mistake or making a fool of yourself, difficulty in rejecting a workable solution and searching for a better one, over-motivation to succeed quickly, fear of supervisors and distrust of colleagues and subordinates, lack of drive in carrying a problem through to completion and test, refusal to take a detour in reaching a goal. Can you recall a time where you let go of an idea all too quickly because of one or more of these blocks?

I have had times in my career where I hid my fears and insecurities of not being good enough along with the need to please and get the job done quickly. I have at times had a fixed mindset on how to do things and found myself saying some of those phrases noted at the start of the chapter. I have many ideas, and when shared with others, I could not understand why they were not as enthusiastic about them as I was! It was frustrating and I let my ideas dissolve because I believed others over me, and I became stagnant. I've since realised the importance of focusing on a few ideas at a time in alliance with my values and the art of effective communication and showing others how my idea will be of value to them – then it will be considered.

Some of the perceptual blocks include difficulty isolating the problem, failure to use all of the senses in observing and difficulty in not investigating the 'obvious'. Some of the cultural blocks include a desire to conform to an accepted pattern, must be practical and economical above all things so that judgement comes into play too quickly, too much faith in reason and logic, too much or too little knowledge about the field that you are working on and belief that indulging in fantasy is a waste of time. Have you been told to 'stop daydreaming', like it's a bad thing?

When I started consulting engineering in Sydney, I noticed there was a disconnect between people and the processes needed for better performance. I got the idea to create a quality assurance guide which stemmed from my experience working in Ireland and processes used there. I'm glad this idea was supported and that I got to execute it. This was over ten years ago, and this guide is still used for onboarding employees and part of compliance documentation when tendering on large projects, so it has had an overall benefit to our practice. If I'd given up too soon, even if there was buy-in, there would be no ongoing benefit.

These blocks surrounding ideation and creation became most evident for me when I became a parent. Having too much faith in reason and logic did not help me when my child was crying, not sleeping, not drinking, and could not tell me why. In the first year of parenting, I hit all the blocks before realising the importance of using all the senses in observing patterns, and that indulging in fantasy was fun! I learned to reinvestigate the 'obvious' when being asked, 'Why is the sky blue? Why do I need to eat vegetables? Why do people die?' There was a new sense of *curiosity* to many of the things in life that I had paid little attention to now in adulthood. The biggest block I came to was when I heard my frustrated words echo back at me from my little toddler, 'Mum, if you don't listen to me you have to go to your room!' It wasn't the worst thing I have said but it resonated with me as I realised I had been forcing my child to listen to me, to conform or else punishment. There was nowhere to hide.

As James Baldwin put it, 'Children have never been very good at listening to their elders, but they have never failed to imitate them.'

I had to change and think of other non-threatening ways to enable my child to learn and grow and *not relinquish their ideas too soon* ...

I have been fortunate enough that my child put a mirror in front of me which made me realise the importance of personal growth and I have regained my enthusiasm for creating within the industry.

Engineers must find new ways to deal with new kinds of problems that will better solve the needs of society. So, do not relinquish your ideas too soon. The advance of creativity in the industry depends on it and at least these two things:

1. **Curiosity** – Be curious and channel your 'childlike' curiosity. Children are not afraid to say what they think or ask questions. They are masters at imagining. They rarely jockey for power in a group and will get straight into building and testing their ideas. Being curious is how we learn what we

don't know, and when we seek, we will find the very thing that will improve what we do.

2. **Personal Development** – Our creativity is only as expansive as we are and the mindset associated with it. Ultimately, we tend to be afraid of ourselves. We place too much value on outer work, as it's measurable, and don't do inner work. We do anything else such as watch TV, listen to music, drink alcohol, hang out with people who remain in their comfort zone, point the finger at others and ignore the three pointing back at us. Being with ourselves our thoughts, emotions, fears and pain is uncomfortable. We need to get comfortable with being uncomfortable. We are horrified by it on an unconscious level because we fear what will come up. We would rather stay on the surface because there's plenty of light there. But the darkness also serves a purpose. A seed needs darkness to sprout. A caterpillar cannot fly if it's not locked inside the cocoon. We won't grow if we refuse to go inside to inspect the condition of our inner world.

There is a massive problem if we focus too much on our outer work and the status quo. It does not make us successful or valuable as humans and it doesn't even make us more successful in general. If we don't have the balance between the inner and outer work, the status quo can deplete our creativity and innovation.

What are the consequences of relinquishing your ideas too soon?

If we all gave up on our ideas, we would lose who we are and what we stand for, and the world would be run by dictators.

There would be people full of regret, there would be less productivity, less resilience, less thinking and much unhappiness. Nothing much, or new, will get created and we will remain stagnant. We will be giving up our freedom.

If you give up, you are giving up the bright future and great results you will get for yourself and society. For example, in 1902 the windshield wiper was invented by a woman who didn't drive. Entrepreneur Mary Anderson thought it made no sense that New York streetcar drivers had to keep jumping off to clean snow from the windshield. At that time, it rarely occurred to anyone else to eliminate the problem. It was something drivers simply accepted and dealt with. It took many years for car manufacturers to see the value of her invention but it was a giant leap forward in vehicle safety design.

The ideas that propel us forward while adapting to ever-**changing** environments are the important ones for the future of the industry.

Ideas? I'm sure you have many ... What do you think it will be like if you don't relinquish your ideas too soon?

ABOUT MARIE O'LOONEY

Marie believes that engineering is one of the most fascinating industries and professions there can be. Whilst there is a long way to go, she sees an industry where engineering is accessible to everyone and there is creativity and innovation embedded in professional practice to address society's needs.

She started her journey decades ago and has had incredible opportunities to advance and deliver award-winning projects and was nominated for the ACSE NSW Female Engineer of the Year in

2021. It wasn't always a straightforward path finding herself in the industry, but she has found it extremely rewarding.

Because of the world of possibility, she is a keen STEAM enthusiast and through mentoring and speaking events she supports creative engineers to be the best that they can be.

Marie is an associate director at SDA Structures and leads by creating space to listen and for sharing of ideas.

Many don't comprehend the gravitas of morality and ethical action and behaviour. Not just thought, but the holistic translation of this into every single practice. Ideologies as such are imperative, as striving for them is uplifting, yet, the reality of building construction is experiencing a fall from grace, as Stan Giaouris explains. Do you not marvel at buildings of past periods and wonder how can they perfectly withstand the test of time, and look at a stock-standard home today, that after a few years, is cracking? Stan's principle remains the bedrock of an industry where everyone wins. Ask yourself, how can you integrate this into every aspect of your work, even when those around you will not? This is how the tide turns.

18

The Pursuit of Craftsmanship in the Australian Construction Industry

BY STAN GIAOURIS

WHAT IS ONE THING YOU WOULD TELL A PERSON?

Embrace ethics, integrity and craftmanship as a core purpose.

WHY?

I marvel daily at our world where skyscrapers reach the heavens and bridges span chasms. The construction industry is both a testament to human achievement and a reflection of our values. It is an arena where every choice, every action, has far-reaching consequences, not just for the structures, but for the very communities we serve and the families we provide shelter for.

As a seasoned expert in the field of building defects, I have devoted my career to solving the intricacies of construction, pushing boundaries and championing the cause of ethical behaviour and craftsmanship within it. If I were tasked with imparting one fundamental piece of advice to guide anyone to succeed in this industry, it would be to embrace ethics, integrity and craftsmanship as your core purpose.

ETHICS AND INTEGRITY

Ethics serve as the guiding compass that steers my decision-making amidst the daily web of challenges, and it remains a steadfast foundation as I strive to achieve my aspirations. It forms the bedrock upon which we must all construct our careers and nurture our characters.

Regardless of what industry you serve, ethical behaviour and integrity will earn you the respect of your peers and the trust of your clients. It will also give you the satisfaction of knowing that your work leaves a legacy, and you will sleep better at night.

The importance of ethics in construction cannot be undervalued, as are providing homes for families. Homeowners will often take out a thirty-year mortgage which is the largest investment they will ever make in their lives. If we get it wrong and deliver a flawed product, this leads to much more than simply financial stress but also affects people's mental health, physical health, relationships and overall wellbeing.

I've personally witnessed the profound impact of ethical conduct within our construction sector. I've seen the devastating aftermath of unethical actions, including shoddy workmanship that shatters people's dreams and forces them out of their homes.

I've observed organisations failing to uphold their commitments, leaving behind a trail of chaos that erodes trust in the entire industry.

On the flipside, I've also had the privilege of experiencing the transformative power of ethical conduct driven by unwavering integrity. It's incredible how it fortifies the very foundations upon which we build, bridges gaps that might otherwise seem insurmountable and constructs not only physical structures but also enduring reputations and relationships.

Ethical conduct in construction manifests in various ways. It means delivering quality work that stands the test of time, honouring promises made to clients and communities and putting safety at the forefront of every project. It involves treating people with respect and fairness. It demands transparency in all dealings, from contracts to finances, and a commitment to environmental sustainability.

In essence, ethical conduct in construction isn't just a moral imperative; it's the cornerstone upon which our industry's credibility and future success rest.

CRAFTSMANSHIP

My journey in the construction industry began in the late 1990s. I was fresh out of high school and full of determination. I took the direct route from school to university, where I pursued a degree in construction management. Unlike many of my peers, I wanted to be right on the ground, learning the ropes from the very beginning. So, while studying at university part-time, I also worked full-time on construction sites across Sydney.

Those early years were tough, working alongside some of

the most resilient individuals I've ever met. In the construction world, they say that they build you up as quickly as they tear you down, and I experienced the truth of that firsthand. My bosses were hard taskmasters, demanding quick thinking, a strong work ethic and a complete lack of attitude. If you couldn't meet those standards, you were out of a job faster than you could blink.

Craftsmanship often goes unnoticed, yet it's a labour of love that demands immense dedication and effort. I've been fortunate to learn the art from exceptional individuals – my mentors who recognised the potential in me when I was young, eager and perhaps somewhat arrogant, or to term it nicer, overly enthusiastic and confident.

Among these mentors, Stephen Flannery at Fugen Construction and Richard Brisland of Brisland Construction played a pivotal role. Their guidance and wisdom shaped my understanding of responsibility, expertise and respect.

Jim Athos, my business partner for nine years at CBS Builders, as well as previously my site manager and project manager earlier in my career. Jim Athos taught me the ropes of the industry, and at the same time challenged me and demonstrated the importance of building strong professional relationships, and above all, doing the right thing. These mentors imparted their knowledge and instilled in me a passion for excellence and a commitment to delivering quality work in every project I undertake.

Today, I've observed a shift in the newer generation of university graduates and young trades entering the construction field. Many seem to lack the hunger and sense of purpose that characterised my own journey. Of course, there are always exceptions, but this realisation inspired me to join the faculty of design, architecture and building at the University of Technology (UTS) as a lecturer. My aim is to inspire the next generation of construction executives and builders to embrace ethics, integrity and the value of craftsmanship.

Throughout my journey spanning over two and a half decades, my driving force has been a passion for positive change and a deep desire to see buildings that endure the test of time. Along the way, I've had the privilege of crossing paths with remarkable individuals who have contributed to my growth in this industry. This collective experience has led to my appointment as the chair of the Master Builders Waterproofing Technical Committee, a role that exemplifies my direct and honest approach to the work we do.

Craftsmanship is like the secret ingredient that elevates a reasonable structure to a great one. Craftsmanship is all about taking pride in the details, making sure the reinforcement is correctly placed, every is cavity drained and every finish flawless. It's the mark of a true professional in our industry.

EARLY CAREER INSIGHTS

My construction career started when I was presented with an opportunity to contribute to the upgrade of key train stations for the Sydney 2000 Olympics. Working on the transformation of Wynyard, Townhall and Central railway stations was a significant milestone that fuelled my purpose to make a meaningful impact in this field. Yet, it wasn't just the architectural and structural transformations that left a lasting impression on me.

During this period, what struck me most was the glaring moral void displayed by the tier one international builder I was employed by. The project, plagued by poor pricing and mis-management from the very beginning, exposed a disheartening pattern – a readiness to exploit subcontractors who operated on verbal instructions and principles of trust, often sealing agreements with nothing more than a handshake. As variations in the project piled up, these honourable subcontractors found themselves driven to financial ruin, while the unscrupulous builders pocketed both their contractual payments and the additional payments for variations whilst sending them to financial ruin. What troubled me the most was that this tactic was not only condoned but also encouraged by senior management.

Being exposed to this at the young age of nineteen made me grow up very quickly; I found my ethical principles were in stark contrast to the behaviours I was witnessing. I couldn't remain silent in the face of such injustices and decided to question the senior contracts manager about these practices, seeking clarity and justice for the subcontractors who were being wronged. Sadly, the response I received was dismissive and aggressive, and it became evident that the company's ethics were fundamentally misaligned with my own.

In the end, I made the difficult decision to resign, but not before gaining a profound life lesson: observe how someone treats others, for eventually, they will treat you the same way. This lesson hit home when the very same company, which thrived on bankrupting subcontractors for profit, treated me with the same disregard by failing to fulfil their commitment to pay my outstanding university fees, a promise made as part of my employment agreement.

These early experiences in the construction industry shaped

not only my professional trajectory but also my commitment to ethical conduct and protecting the wellbeing of those I work with. This experience serves as a constant reminder that in an industry driven by integrity, trust and respect, we all have a responsibility to uphold these values and ensure that everyone is treated justly and with respect.

CAREER ANCHORED IN ETHICS

When I reflect on the early days of my career, I can't deny that those struggles were instrumental in shaping who I am today. In fact, the journey has been marked by challenges and important lessons that ultimately helped me refine my moral compass and understand the true value of ethics.

After my initial employment was soured by unscrupulous practices, I actively sought out leaders who operated with integrity, recognising that this often meant firm but always fair leadership.

My career decisions led me to Fugen Constructions, a highly respected tier two builder in the industry. It was here that I obtained next-level hands-on experience that would prove to be invaluable in shaping my construction expertise. I willingly took on a range of site tasks and roles, from demolition, concreting, to finishing work. I worked alongside tradespeople who were experienced and competent; they taught me how to channel my pride into my work and to serve others. My time at Fugen Constructions was truly a happy and rewarding one, where I was able to merge my practical experience with the theoretical knowledge I was learning at university.

PASSION FOR QUALITY AND STANDARDS

From the outset of my career to the present day, I've observed a persistent gap in the understanding and application of codes and standards among various stakeholders in the construction industry, including tradespeople, building experts, builders, developers and even architects. It's important to recognise that this deficiency extends far beyond surface-level concerns; it carries profound and far-reaching implications for the industry as a whole.

First and foremost, the lack of awareness and adherence to codes and standards jeopardises the safety of construction projects. Failure to meet these standards can result in structural vulnerabilities, compromising the wellbeing of occupants and the public. Furthermore, it can lead to costly legal issues, disputes and liabilities for all parties involved. In turn, this erodes trust, making it difficult to establish enduring reputations and foster client confidence.

Additionally, the failure to keep pace with evolving codes and standards hinders innovation and progress within the industry. It stifles opportunities for efficiency improvements, environmentally sustainable practices and the incorporation of advanced building materials and technologies. This not only impacts the industry's competitiveness but also its ability to adapt to changing societal needs and expectations.

This observation has inspired me to advocate for change and to bridge this dangerous gap. To illustrate my point, several years ago when a timber deck I had constructed for a friend began to warp, I was curious to find out why. In accordance with the teachings I had received from my past site manager, I had ensured a minimum of 150 millimetres of clearance under the bearers and joists. However, when I reviewed this against the National Construction Code it revealed a different requirement: 150 millimetres at one end and a substantial 400 millimetres at the other. My friend's deck was created incorrectly due to the uniform 150 millimetres I had implemented, serving as a stark reminder of the need for precise adherence to evolving standards. This resulted in excess moisture in the subfloor, and the timber deck cupping.

To this day there is resistance among seasoned professionals to embrace new practices and standards. It is disheartening to encounter individuals proudly asserting, 'I've been doing this for thirty years and this is how I do it.' I firmly believe that our industry is in a constant state of evolution, demanding ongoing education, participation in seminars, networking and a thorough understanding of emerging building products, their strengths, weaknesses and compliance with codes and standards. It is my mission to advocate for these principles and drive positive change within our field.

BUILDING FOR THE FUTURE

My deep commitment to ethical construction practices extends far beyond personal belief; it is embedded in a profound sense of responsibility. When individuals or families commit to a **thirty**-year mortgage on a property, it becomes our duty as builders to deliver a structure that will endure for those three decades with minimal maintenance. I emphasise the paramount importance of craftsmanship and integrity in fulfilling this ethical imperative.

In my view, the construction industry plays a pivotal role in society by providing the fundamental necessities that distinguish developed nations from developing ones: shelter, clean water and electricity. Constructing flawed and structurally compromised buildings, prone to issues like moisture and leaking issues, is tantamount to a failure in this vital societal role. It underscores an uncomfortable truth – when builders deliver substandard structures, they deny people the very shelter they've entrusted us to provide.

My vision transcends individual projects and embraces the increasing legislation that is permeating the industry. I view this development as a positive step forward, a mechanism that will eventually sift out those lacking competence and adequate training, especially those who have casually used the title of 'builder'. For too long, the term has been diluted, diminishing its significance. I eagerly anticipate the day when identifying as a builder will be held to the same rigorous standards and esteem as the titles of architect or engineer. This transformation is not merely a desire but a necessity for the betterment of our industry and the wellbeing of those we serve.

ABOUT STAN GIAOURIS

Stan Giaouris' distinguished career in the construction industry is driven by his dedication, unwavering principles and an unrelenting pursuit of quality. He stands as a champion for ethical construction practices, embodying the values he holds dear. Stan's journey is a testament to the significance of ethical conduct in the construction industry, serving as a beacon of inspiration for all those who aspire to leave a lasting mark in the realm of craftsmanship.

Stan encourages all individuals in the industry to never cease learning. He holds a university degree and has recently achieved accreditation as a builder certifier. In addition, he possesses a Certificate III in Construction Waterproofing. Stan's commitment to education and industry advancement is evident through his role as a lecturer at the University of Technology Sydney (UTS) within the esteemed faculty of design, architecture and building since 2018.

Beyond his academic achievements, Stan has taken on pivotal industry roles and holds various qualifications:

- *Chairperson Master Builders Waterproofing Technical Committee.*
- *NSW Fair Trading Builders Licence #188343C since 2006.*
- *D&BPA Reg Building Practitioner BUP#000624.*
- *Registered Strata Bond Scheme Inspector (ASBC) #131.*
- *Registered Liveable Housing Design Assessor #20030.*
- *Lecturer at UTS in the Faculty of Design, Architecture and Building since 2018.*
- *President of St George division of the Master Builders Association.*
- *Councillor for the Master Builders Association of NSW.*

Stan Giaouris' contributions extend far beyond his impressive qualifications, making him an influential figure in our industry and an inspiration to all.

In each interaction I've had the pleasure of having with Kabri Lehrman-Schmid, there's a deep sense of responsibility that emanates from her exemplary leadership. A deep sense of pride and ownership that she seeks to uphold in each interaction for the greater good. An industry leader as such who has cultivated such immense conscious awareness is rare, especially with a track record of successful megaproject delivery. And one who is able to have each individual on her site front of mind. How? What is the secret that enables sites to not be chaotic, but a symphony orchestra? Kabri, in true nature, gives all for everyone to win.

19

WE ARE ALL GATEKEEPERS

BY KABRI LEHRMAN-SCHMID

WHAT IS ONE THING YOU WOULD TELL A PERSON?

You are a gatekeeper of resources and opportunities. Every interaction and technical task presents a choice: will you inhibit your teammates' access or establish a culture of generous collaboration and shared success? By adopting a gatekeeper mindset, you gain the power to shape your career growth, your team's success and even the future of the industry.

WHY?

As a superintendent for a large general contractor, my vision is to lead projects built on accuracy, transparency, mutual respect and shared success. My position gives me significant influence over my projects, functioning as a bridge for information exchange between my clients, designers and trade partners (tier subcontractors). I am directly responsible for decisions that impact the project's progress. This pressure makes me acutely aware that how I communicate and delegate work establishes the prevailing behavioural norms of the jobsite, i.e. how my crews receive and execute work. These responsibilities require my constant consideration to which information and resources I will share.

Maintaining a gatekeeper mindset ensures I stay accountable to my vision of project leadership. Symbolic keys in hand, I am conscious of how my actions either facilitate progress, collaboration and innovation, or block these opportunities. Effectively motivating my teammates to enthusiastically participate is what makes my projects uniquely successful, fulfilling and memorable.

Consider, for example, the missed opportunities we might discover in a Monday morning jobsite meeting: My electrician is frustrated they cannot install their in-slab conduit because the ironworkers continued placing reinforcing bars through the weekend to meet the concrete schedule. The work will not be completed in time for the electrical inspection. Had I arranged to walk the deck with all crews before the weekend, we would have discussed these conflicts and learned the expectations of each crew. We could've created mutual success by resequencing the flow of Saturday's reinforcing to retain access to essential electrical runs. And our understanding of the work's urgency could have been informed by the electrician's willingness to exercise their rapport with the inspector – who might have agreed to reschedule. Instead, the concrete schedule is at risk, electricians are overstaffed (and unwilling to exercise their favours), and the ironworkers might need to remove bars – bad for morale, business and the week's start.

My ability to effectively manage risk and develop strategies that account for the perspective of each participant relies on the fundamental understanding that the plan must be informed by insights from others. This is a key function of my role as a superintendent – smart (and safe) coordination. I know I've done my job well if the outcome of my plan enables teammates and employees to recognise their individual contributions to the team's success!

WE ARE ALL GATEKEEPERS

As gatekeepers, we each control access to knowledge, logistics, relationships and respect. No matter our title or role, our behaviours and choices throughout the workday will have positive or negative impacts on our teams.

At our best, we exhibit characteristics like generosity, trust, encouragement and curiosity. We create incredible opportunities to:

- Facilitate exceptional communication on our project teams.
- Emphasise quality that results in personal pride and client satisfaction.
- Motivate production, engagement and empowerment of our people.
- Foster innovation that drives financial success.
- Build psychological safety on our teams to expand our perspectives.
- Enhance the greater perception of our industry to attract future talent.

On the flip side, when we exhibit traits such as egotism, intimidation, suspicion or criticism, we jeopardise trust, hinder growth and perpetuate harmful biases. Withholding resources stifles progress, limits employee desire for advancement, and leads to rework and frustration.

DAILY APPLICATION

In the midst of our projects, we're constantly juggling intricate details, navigating procurement processes, chasing financial targets and managing relationships. Without a clear road map towards our vision of both personal career growth and team success, it's easy to get bogged down in the whirlwind of shifting priorities and the roller-coaster of emotions on the jobsite.

If we wholeheartedly embrace our role as gatekeepers, our actions gain a new sense of purpose. All those technical tasks we handle on a daily basis? They're our chance to foster a culture of open communication that values resource sharing and skill development.

When we truly understand how much our projects' success relies on our own accountability, we start making decisions that shape how our team tackles challenges, strengthens partnerships and sparks genuine enthusiasm for our project goals. Consider how the following strategies could be implemented in your next team meeting:

- **Establish your expectations for engagement**. Use clear language to let others know you value honest communication. Create opportunities for everyone to speak, defend their right to participate and then validate understanding.
- **Share your knowledge generously**. Demonstrate your commitment to a collaborative approach by providing either the

broader context of a task ('big picture') or delving into its intricate details. This, in turn, motivates others to contribute their insights and expertise, leading to more precise planning and cooperative issue resolution.

- **Acknowledge the importance of empathy.** Seek to understand your teammates' processes, their preferred modes of communication and their definition of success. Your awareness of their perspective will inspire trust that results in more effective and enthusiastic execution of work.

- **Role model your commitments to others**. Show genuine respect for the relationships you have with your teammates. Their perception of your trustworthiness will have a significant impact on their willingness to trust you in the future.

- **Showcase the impact of participation.** Reflect on methods to underscore the results shaped by the input of others. Even mentioning small examples of refining a plan or resolving an issue can greatly substantiate your commitment to fostering participation and transparency. Similarly, demonstrating gratitude and normalising the discussion of mistakes serve as remarkable techniques for fostering two-way communication.

Being a gatekeeper in an industry focused on production means we can't afford to have a narrow, transactional mindset. Our approach should be fuelled by a persistent and sincere curiosity of processes and perspectives. This identity matters because it aligns us with the core values of our industry: taking pride in our work, passing on knowledge through apprenticeships and serving our families and communities. These shared values act as both the driving force and the binding agent for our teams.

It's essential to highlight that this broader perspective empowers us to challenge traditional biases, industry-specific stigmas and negative perceptions by incorporating topics of inclusion, mental health and psychological safety into our daily operations. As gatekeepers, our influence extends beyond proficient planning, delegation and execution – it encompasses acknowledging the humanity of our teammates by actively embodying partnership, overseeing the exchange of information and nurturing relationships within the wider project team.

WHOLE TEAM IMPACT

Adopting a gatekeeper mindset benefits all project participants, including owners, designers, contractors and their crews. When everyone comes to the table with an understanding of their own resources and a common expectation to collaborate generously, the team fosters a culture that values each other's achievements and integrated problem-solving.

Each party can adopt strategies that centre shared project success and each will realise unique advantages from this approach.

OWNERS/CLIENTS

Owners play a vital role as the ultimate gatekeepers with resources such as money, time and decision-making power. Their greatest opportunity to influence the project outcome is to clearly establish the baseline expectations for team performance and relationships. This can be accomplished through both contracting strategy and the modelling of desired behaviours.

To leverage their authority, owner and client team members

should:

- Recognise their ability to clearly set expectations for engagement, communication and conflict resolution.
- Model the relationships they want their architect, engineer and contractor team to build.
- Choose to demonstrate flexibility and creativity within or beyond the limitations of their processes.

DESIGNERS/ENGINEERS

Design teams are the source of essential project knowledge and often play a primary role in decision-making. However, communication inefficiencies can hinder their ability to accurately translate the owner's vision into buildable documents that align with the project's budget goals.

To enhance project communication, design professionals should:

- Place emphasis on ensuring the owner and stakeholders understand and validate concepts.
- Foster a habit of openly discussing design process constraints to encourage collaborative problem-solving within the team.
- Engage contractors for constructability analysis and to draw lessons from previous experiences.

GENERAL CONTRACTORS

By recognising their key role as gatekeepers for jobsite processes, logistics, construction budget and schedule float, general contractors stand to benefit from the increased participation, productivity and safer practices of their tier subcontractors and skilled tradespeople. Given these contractual arrangements, general contractors bear the greatest opportunity and responsibility to cultivate jobsite cultures that encourage improved communication, innovative approaches to problem-solving and the retention of their skilled workforce. Let's consider the potential for impact:

- Trade Partners/Tier Subcontractors:

    Trade partners bring specialised skill sets and essential material resources to projects. Unfortunately, it is often the case that tier subcontractors are accustomed to being treated poorly by general contractors who wrongly believe that withholding information gives them more control over project outcomes.

    To build back trust and support the success of their tier subcontractors as partners, contractors should:
    - Model respect and integrity during conversations about other contractors by demonstrating appreciation for their contributions.
    - Collaborate to solve problems and find solutions together.
    - Display curiosity and take action to prioritise the success of their subcontractors.
    - Provide considerate and timely responses to extend opportunities for accurate planning and quality work.

- Skilled Tradespeople:

    The workers putting the work in place should be treated

with the utmost dignity and be personally considered when deciding your allocation of resources and information. Leaders who invest in the management or development of skilled tradespeople have an incredible privilege to influence both the success of individual workers and the holistic advancement of the construction industry.

To actively support workers in the field, leadership should:

- Demonstrate respect for their contributions and reward teaching behaviours.
- Actively solicit feedback to continuously enhance onsite worker experiences and tackle any issues that arise (follow up is key!).
- Invest in the workforce's future by offering training and educational opportunities that cultivate an expectation of inclusivity and achievement.

In the role of gatekeeper, each of us holds the power to influence the dynamics of our project teams. When we intentionally encourage collaboration and generously share resources, we establish an environment in which team success, collective problem-solving and mutual trust are held in high regard. Yet, our impact as gatekeepers can stretch far beyond the boundaries of our current projects. We're presented with the transformative opportunity to use our influence with intention and effect substantial change – granting us the power to sculpt our professional journeys, build resilient teams and propel the course of our industry's future to new heights.

ABOUT KABRI LEHRMAN-SCHMID

Over her impressive sixteen-year career, Kabri Lehrman-Schmid has established herself as a trailblazing superintendent for Hensel Phelps in the United States. She has set new standards for the influence of field leadership on her design-build teams, while passionately endorsing industry initiatives aimed at enhancing workforce well-being. Her $1.9 billion portfolio highlights her adept management across all phases of progressive delivery projects within the transportation and higher education sectors. Kabri's contributions have been acknowledged with multiple honours, including recognition as one of Engineering News-Record's *2023 National Top 20 Under 40 professionals, featured on* Construction Business Owner's *2019 cover for 20 Outstanding Women in Construction and as the inaugural recipient of AGC of Washington's 2022 Rising Star Award. Kabri advocates for the potential of field management in tackling biases and mental health stigmas within the construction industry and is a dedicated contributor to training programs aimed at elevating leadership skill sets among forepersons.*

If you do not consciously seek to abide by the next winning principle, you will lose it all. And all is yourself. There is no you. There cannot be any you when the notion of you is simply random constructs provided by everyone else but you. Why do you strive to be like everyone else, when most people don't know who they are or where they are going? Do you think that you weren't already given everything you need as an individual, that you must shut that down and put on a cloak that the industry told you to? For you are not your job title, your project, your hometown, your religion, your degree (definitely do not seek to attach your identity to a paper) and you are not even your name. When you shed all this, are you able to define yourself? Those who reject convention in the pursuit of different always win. Rachael Keeble propositions you: individualisation or conformity. Before you make the decision, understand her winning principle.

20

WHY EXCELLENCE LIES IN CHAMPIONING INDIVIDUALITY OVER CONFORMITY

BY RACHAEL KEEBLE

WHAT IS ONE THING YOU WOULD TELL A PERSON?
Choose individuality over conformity.

WHY?
It will come as no surprise that construction is frequently represented as a homogenous industry. It has a reputation for being old-fashioned and physically demanding with a macho culture. But to characterise the industry only in this way is unfairly reductive. At a base economic level, the industry contributes to 10% of global GDP and employs about 7% of the global workforce.

The construction industry is growing and changing. Not all of us wear steel-capped boots.

When you join the industry, it can be tempting to simply want to fit in – to choose conformity over individuality. It is normal human nature in an environment where the influence of colleagues and peers often plays a major role in the advancement of our careers. The industry is also heavily regulated by standards and codes, with projects that involve compliance, complex hierarchies, tight budgets and time frames and moderate-to-no appetite for risk. All of which generally results in little room for innovation, creativity or experimentation.

The deepest problem with the construction industry is that we are made to believe that we have to 'fit in'. The high-pressure, fast-paced culture can squeeze the passion and optimism out of new joiners in favour of conformity. They are told 'this is the way it has always been done' or that they need to 'serve their time' and climb the corporate ladder. All this results in individuals leaving the industry at rates we cannot keep up with. If people cannot bring their whole selves to work, they are unlikely to want long-term careers in the sector.

But for the industry to accelerate its rate of change, we need people that are unafraid to be themselves and voice their opinions – and we need the industry to be welcoming of this. When people can come to work as their full selves, innovation and creativity will thrive, diversity of the workforce will increase and positive change will happen. The construction industry faces serious challenges to keep up with the rate of global change and this requires new ways of thinking, designing and building.

For years, I felt compelled to stay in my lane and was fearful of popping my head above the parapet. I diligently got on with my job, but feeling the whole time that there was more that I could contribute and more of myself that I could bring to work. I am a deeply creative person who adores working with people, empowering them, writing, teaching and learning but these were not skills I could use in the ways that I wanted in the conventional pathways within the sector. I could see firsthand a desperate need for my wider skill set in the industry but could not see how I could use them in a way that would be accepted and embraced.

In the last few years, I have leaned into my individuality and done what the general narrative of the industry tells us we cannot do. I applied, aged thirty-two, to become a trustee of the CIOB, one of the largest global charities for construction industry professionals, and was successfully appointed. I started my own newsletter in which I write monthly on how we can build better. I took a career break to travel some of the world and refocus on my beliefs, values and priorities so I could better incorporate them into my life and work. I put myself forward to speak at and contribute to industry leading events.

And most importantly, I set up my own company, BuiltWell Project Management, which helps others in the industry learn how to level up and confidently step away from conformity and into courageous industry career paths. By empowering, educating and uplifting others I feel like my work is aligned with my greater life ambition of making the world a better place. And by giving other people a framework to do the same, I have become deeply connected to a cycle of accelerating positive change in the industry where embracing individuality is becoming the norm.

I was recently at an industry event, and I asked a group of talented professionals what they were passionate about. It took a few blinks for the question to register before one guy admitted he was an ardent tattooist. He rolled up his trouser leg to show the most beautiful and intricate designs that he had carefully (and painfully!) inked into his skin. Another man told us he played the saxophone in a local jazz band. A woman said she ran ultramarathons on her annual leave. One admitted he did not know what he was passionate about, but that he did enjoy spending time with his dog. These admissions were made in the hushed tones of people confessing to guilty pastimes. But we all have unique qualities and passions, and we deserve the right to be proud of them inside and outside of work. Why can't individuality be celebrated over conformity?

The reality is that it is not easy to choose individuality over conformity in our industry. Construction is highly regulated, and a level of conformity and standardisation will always be required. For this reason, it can be hard to get the balance right and to know when it is appropriate to challenge the accepted norm. Plus, coming to work as your full self takes courage, confidence and the release of other people's expectations. But doesn't excellence always lie at the heart of debate, innovation and challenge? In my career it has taken me too long to realise that turning up as myself IS my unique selling point. That the industry needs exactly what I have to offer and that being authentically me in my work is necessary so I can help make the industry a better place.

So, if I could tell a person in the construction industry one thing, it would be to choose individuality over conformity. Embrace your quirks and abilities, and bring all your unique qualities to work. Carve out your niche of excellence in the industry and encourage others to do the same. Take time to work out and establish your beliefs and values and align your work with these ambitions. By doing so, you will create your own ripple effect and become part of the movement that is positively changing the industry from the inside out.

ABOUT RACHAEL KEEBLE

Rachael Keeble is a project management specialist with ten years' construction industry experience. She is the founder of BuiltWell Project Management, providing high-impact training that teaches project managers how to lead authentically, become star performers and deliver exceptional project outcomes.

Rachael is a trustee of the Chartered Institute of Buildings, author of How Can We Build Better? *and mentors young women navigating their early careers. Recognising the tough conditions within the construction industry, she is dedicated to providing the tools and coaching necessary to flourish in these circumstances. Rachael's mission is to educate and empower the current and future project management workforce so they can level up, build long-term career success and become confident leaders.*

Do you ever look at someone and think to yourself,
What is going through their mind right now?
*Clearly, nothing, which is reflective of them missing
an essential quality of leadership. Wally Adamchik
shares a secret of leadership that you would think
would really be more common. Alas, many 'leaders'
who lack this quality are a big cause of the causalities
experienced in the industry on many levels. The
excellence of leadership and its impact on the industry
cannot truly rise until each takes on this principle,
and remember, what may be simple to do, is also
simple not to do. What could it be …*

21

SELF-AWARENESS

BY WALLY ADAMCHIK

WHAT IS ONE THING YOU WOULD TELL A PERSON?

If you are to lead others, you must first be able to lead yourself. To do that, you must become an expert on you. Self-awareness is the key to any real success.

WHY?

You will often read that leadership is not about you. It is about the ones you seek to lead and influence; it is a social process. I have uttered those words myself. Well, I was wrong. It is all about you. It starts with you, and it ends with you. It starts when you dare to answer, *Why am I the way I am?* It ends when your team achieves great things, and you step aside as they bask in the glow of that achievement.

Leadership is a story of your nature (your DNA), combined with your nurture (your upbringing). Dr Lanny Hass, Professor Emeritus at North Carolina State University, calls it a 'Momma's house' story. Our early experiences (while living in our momma's house) profoundly impact our behaviour for the rest of our life. Your DNA is your wiring; your upbringing is your programming. But with self-awareness, you can install new software.

This inner journey to self-awareness means being in control of our emotions, thoughts and actions. We do not want to give in to knee-jerk reactions in difficult situations; we want to respond calmly and thoughtfully. We understand that just because they ping, doesn't mean we have to pong. In fact, there is great power in this pause, if you can harness it.

Michael Nichols, PhD, takes a bit further: 'If you don't listen to yourself, it's unlikely that anyone else will. Listening to yourself means not only respecting your own feelings, but also getting to know something about your style of communicating.'

The goal is to earn a PhD in *you*. You will have accomplished this when you:

- Understand your thoughts, feelings, values and background and how they impact decision-making and relationships.
- Recognise your own biases by tracing them to their origins.
- Accept yourself.
- Intentionally seek a new way forward. You discover new ways of thinking and acting when situations become difficult or uncertain, or in times of urgency.

This self-awareness delivers self-esteem, which leads to self-confidence. Self-esteem refers to your appreciation and value for yourself. Your self-esteem develops and changes as a result of your life experiences and interactions with other people. Ideally, it builds over time and enables greater action. Self-confidence is your belief in yourself and your abilities. This can fluctuate, depending on the situation. It's normal to feel quite confident in some circumstances and less so in others. But in general, self-confidence should increase over time. This enables us to better meet life's challenges.

American author Joseph Campbell chronicles the hero's journey in which 'a hero [you] ventures forth from the world of common day to day into a region of supernatural wonder: fabulous forces are there encountered and a decisive victory is won: the hero comes back from this mysterious adventure with the power to bestow boons on his fellow man'. This journey is uniquely yours into your inner realm.

As a people, we have known this for eons. The wisdom of Chinese military general and philosopher Sun Tzu, the insight of Buddha, the introspection of Marcus Aurelius, the universal practicality of Indigenous peoples worldwide and the enlighten-ment of any spiritual text is there for the taking. We are called to greatness. Sadly, most of us do not heed the call to become self-aware. So close, yet so far.

I was feeling pretty good about these insights as I wrote them. The concepts were familiar to me, and I was happy about the opportunity to pull them together. But then I had one of those moments of clarity and realised I was sending you down a path of self-discovery that would lead to a dead end. What next?

Knowledge without action is wasted. A new path awaits. The real success comes, not simply when you know you, but when you do something with what you know. We have all met peo-ple who can accurately tell you about themselves, but then do nothing with that knowledge. I see it all the time in coaching. A person will take an assessment, we debrief the results, and they remark, 'I already knew that.'

Then I ask, 'What are you doing about it? How are you leveraging your strengths? How are you working to ensure your weaknesses do not derail you?' Silence. These people don't really want to know themselves. They prefer to judge rather than learn. They choose automatic reactions based on old programming, rather than a thoughtful choice to work toward something better. Their self-awareness is superficial. They have not done the real work to understand, therefore they are unable to take real action and move toward that better future.

Coming to terms with one's imperfection, working to beat the demons down, learning to excel at what you were put on this earth to do, is where the real challenge lies. The pay-off is worth it. You emerge from your journey transformed, with the power and confidence to transform others.

ABOUT WALLY ADAMCHIK

Wally Adamchik is the president of FireStarter Speaking and Consulting, a US-based consultancy focused on leadership in the construction industry. With experience in construction (his father and brother were tradesmen), the military and corporate America, you get an honest expert who understands the multinational as well as he does the family-owned company. Since 2003, he has supported some of the most notable firms in construction and is a regular presenter at industry gatherings. Author of No Yelling: The Nine Secrets of Marine Corps Leadership *and* Construction Leadership from A to Z; 26 Words to Lead By. *He holds the certified speaking professional and certified management consultant designations.*

Every moment you are given a choice as to the experience of yourself you wish someone else can have of you. That is wholly in your control. So, what do you wish that experience to be like? I not-so-fondly recall the purposeful disempowering and political plays experienced during my time in corporate construction, which always begged the question, why? What's the point of robbing someone else of their power, why would someone make this their main focus? I took a radical approach to reclaiming my self-power, but unfortunately, there remain many who are still at the hand of unethical power plays in the industry – for what gain exactly, it remains unknown. David G Fisher is the co-author who has the most decades of experience to his name out of all of us here, and it's safe to say, has seen a myriad of situations and thousands of conversations. There's a not-so-secret secret that he has stood for and now imparts to you, so everyone can win.

22

EMPOWERING OTHERS FOR SUCCESS

BY DAVID G FISHER

WHAT IS ONE THING YOU WOULD TELL A PERSON?

Seek to empower others instead of detracting from them.

WHY?

If you are a leader, I would ask you to reflect on your style of leadership. How do you engage with your team? I believe as a true leader, it is not about commanding people, it's about unleashing their true potential and providing the support and tools to equip them to grow and fly like eagles. We can either empower someone to greatness and have the best team, where we as the leader can feel very proud of their achievements, or we can disempower our team and slowly destroy everything around us.

Even if you don't currently hold a leadership position by title, you can still act on this principle by taking on your responsibilities with support and dedication for whatever function you're currently carrying in a team. For example, if you have just started in the industry, put in the hard yards, do the simple tasks well without complaining, give it all that you have, don't look for glory, wait for your turn to step up. If you can't do the small things well, you will never handle the greater things. Sometimes we don't see the big picture of how a company works or the issues behind the curtain of the project with the client.

The core idea is that empowering leadership unlocks people's talents and drives better results than authoritarian control. By sharing power and showing confidence in our people, I would say, a great leader magnifies what the team can achieve together.

Empowerment, as a concept, holds immense potential. It's the idea that we can lift each other up, fostering an environment where individuals can flourish and reach their full potential. It's the belief that we can create a workplace where everyone's voice is valued and where hierarchies do not stifle innovation and growth.

However, the sad truth is that empowerment is often nothing more than a buzzword, splashed across motivational posters and corporate mission statements. The reality we face is often starkly different from the inspiring message. Let me share a story to illustrate this disheartening gap.

Picture a bustling construction site, where dreams are built and structures rise towards the sky. At first glance, it's a place filled with potential, a place where every worker should feel valued and empowered. But as we delve deeper into the narrative, the truth unveils itself like a dark cloud over the sun.

In this setting, we have a crane onsite. Jack is the crane operator and George is the dogman, who performs the essential role of directing the crane operator during the lift. George communicates with the crane operator during each lift to direct the load and help the operator accurately shift the load when it's out of the operator's view.

They go to many sites around the city and they work day after day, giving their best, always thinking about safety, making sure everyone goes home to their families and loved ones at night.

They both work together, have dreams for their families and loved ones, of making an impact on the safety of the industry. They believe that they should be heard when they know something is not right, however the harsh reality is that Jack and George find themselves in a culture where their voices are not encouraged – but rather silenced. They witness the power plays that are as common as the concrete under our boots. The site management team dictates decisions based on cost, they belittle Jack the crane operator and all his fellow workers because he won't do what they say.

The very essence of empowerment, which should nurture growth and safety on the sites, is twisted into a culture of disrespect, poisoning the well of collaboration and creating an atmosphere of mistrust.

This story serves as a poignant reminder of the challenges we face in achieving true empowerment. It highlights the emotional toll that a disempowering environment can take on individuals like Jack and his fellow workers. It's a call to action, a plea to bridge the gap between the promise and the reality, and to create a workplace where empowerment is not just a word on a poster but a living, breathing force that propels us all towards a brighter future.

Another story I would like to share is in the bustling office within the construction industry, where plans and dreams converged, there was a young CA, let's call her Sarah. She has a heart full of passion and a mind brimming with innovative ideas, she joined the team with high hopes. She believed in the power of collaboration and the potential for her voice to make a difference.

However, as weeks turned into months, Sarah's enthusiasm began to wane. She noticed that her voice, once so eager and vibrant, was slowly being silenced. In meetings, her ideas were often met with dismissive glances and polite nods, only to be promptly forgotten. The voices of those with more senior titles drowned out hers, and she felt like an insignificant cog in a vast machine.

One day, she mustered the courage to share an idea she believed could revolutionise a critical project. She presented it with enthusiasm, hoping for support and collaboration. But instead, she was met with scepticism and resistance. Some colleagues even whispered behind her back, casting doubt on her abilities.

As Sarah's confidence eroded, she found herself withdrawing from the very conversations and interactions that once fuelled her passion. She no longer felt valued or heard, and her belief in empowerment had been replaced by disillusionment.

This story is not unique, for in many workplaces, the promise of empowerment often gives way to the harsh reality of hierarchical power, dynamics and ego-driven decisions. It is a stark reminder that true empowerment requires more than just words on a poster; it demands a genuine commitment to valuing every voice and fostering an environment where individuals can thrive.

It's a story that resonates with many, for it reflects the universal yearning for a workplace where empowerment is not just a concept but a lived experience – a place where every voice matters, and the potential of everyone is recognised and nurtured.

Within the construction industry, disempowerment thrives through pervasive behaviours that eat away at the very fabric of the workplace. It's a place where voices are silenced, where gaslighting and rumour-spreading are used as weapons against colleagues. Titles become instruments of power, resulting in uncalled-for power plays and a glaring power imbalance. Individuals are disrespected for no reason other than the perception of their position.

True empowerment, on the other hand, demands a different approach. It begins with giving everyone a voice and genuinely listening, not just to their words, but also to their best interests and concerns. It requires us to believe in each person's potential, rejecting the confines of hierarchy and power struggles. Empowerment entails adopting a mindset of servitude, not to demean but to add value to others' lives. It hinges on shedding our egos, replacing assumptions with genuine questions that reveal the truth within someone.

Moreover, empowerment isn't a one-way street. It also involves empowering yourself. This means standing up for your beliefs with humility and perspective. It's about learning to move forward without losing faith in yourself and cultivating deep expertise that makes you invaluable.

In the face of challenges, you may lose everything, but your knowledge, skills and passion remain. Thus, working on these three aspects – knowledge, skills and passion – is pivotal to your empowerment. Having forty-three years of experience has allowed me to consistently find resilience in any situation.

In conclusion, it's crucial to acknowledge that if you find yourself in a disempowered situation, you need to take action to change it. If you have the responsibility of empowering others, introspect on your behaviours. While the norm may seem like a state of empowerment, the reality often proves vastly different.

Our way forward is to reclaim genuine empowerment, where voices are heard, hierarchies are dismantled and egos are set aside.

So, I leave you with a question: Are you willing to take on the full responsibility of empowerment, even if it means going against the industry's grain? The answer may hold the key to a brighter, more empowering future for all.

ABOUT DAVID G FISHER

David, a seasoned veteran with forty-three years of experience spanning two countries, paints a vivid picture of the construction industry. He describes it as a place where knowledge is gained from the grand masters of the trade, from the trade school activities to the ivy-clad towers of the universities.

He learnt from the school of life, a business of hard knocks, where humble beginnings were formed from each brick laid, each beam hoisted, the ever-expanding problems and challenges that he faced, crafting his identity from the sweat and grit that moulds all our souls today.

With lessons etched deep, the fires of experience from the failures and struggles, he embraces wisdom and compassion. He now stands as a custodian with forty-three years under his belt, both as a home builder and a commercial builder, to unveil the concept of empowerment where a new chapter and legacy will be delivered.

Aren't we all walking around as shot nervous systems? Coty Leigh Fournier brings a radical perspective to a stale conversation when it comes to people behind the projects. That notion was new a few years ago, but now, what do most actually mean by that? In equal measure, I had to examine that myself. Deeply consider how our interactions with others daily can evolve with the application of this principle. Do you think this falls into the realm of our individual responsibility? Think deeply about why this gift of a secret has been presented to you by Coty, and how you can best serve through its application. I hope you're ready for it, as I certainly wasn't when I'd first forayed into the secret …

23

EVERYTHING'S GONNA BE ALRIGHT

BY COTY LEIGH FOURNIER

WHAT IS ONE THING YOU WOULD TELL A PERSON?

You must help everyone to feel less afraid.

WHY?

The construction management industry has passed its competitive tipping point, as the basic qualifications of elite contractors in any given marketplace or area of specialisation are converging to relative equality. When comparing legitimate 'apples-to-apples' competitors, you will find, for the most part, they can (and will) lay equal claim to the most touted outcomes. If you don't believe me, take a hard look at a handful of their marketing materials and listen carefully to what they say about themselves in a formal sales presentation or brief elevator pitch. You will quickly discern that everyone professes the same six qualifications, floating amidst a sea of well-intended polish and decoration – but when you boil it all down, everyone sounds something like this:

We deliver (1) top-quality construction projects, (2) on time and (3) on budget, with excellent (4) safety outcomes. Here are some relevant (5) client testimonials from projects that are very similar to yours to prove it. How do we do it? We have the (6) best people.

No-one likes to hear this, but the reason everyone sounds pretty much the same is because everyone IS pretty much the same. This familiar collection of desirable qualifications is essential, but no longer differentiates between legitimate competitors. You simply cannot improve upon the basics of construction management skills and deliverables enough to have it mean anything anymore. The incremental returns are diminishing and often zero.

This leaves our industry's decision-makers in earnest search for meaningful differentiation amongst today's elite construction companies. And in that search, there is a coveted prize that is rarely spoken of out loud. It's hiding in plain sight at the intersection of construction management and a famous quote by Dr Maya Angelou:

'I've learned that people will forget what you said, and people will forget what you did, but people will never forget how you made them feel.'

Her words aren't simply words to live by. They are words to work by, in virtually any industry. In the construction industry, however, they are especially insightful as much more than a moral compass. They represent a critical mind-shift that the most successful companies use to turn a unique industry problem into a competitive advantage. And it goes something like this.

As construction managers, we live in a world of estimations and educated projections, coupled with the responsibility of managing unpredictable groups of people and the coordination of an exhausting number of pieces and parts – that are all subject to change at any time. At best, we all do our best to make informed decisions, draft a solid game plan, adjust it as required, solve ever-emerging problems and move the ball one step closer to the contracted deliverables. However, truth be told, when a construction company begins a project, the only thing they can say with any certainty is that nothing will go down exactly like it was planned. There are just too many variables and unknowns associated with everything and everyone. It's an imperfect process, even for the very best construction companies who employ exceptionally trained construction managers. Therefore, despite herculean effort, we find ourselves working from directions, assumptions, estimates and schedules that require constant adjustment – the consequences of which then need to be effectively managed and communicated to the highest possible understanding and satisfaction for all project stakeholders. What's interesting is that occasionally something that gets said or done ends up being 100% dead wrong and way off track – but most of the time, it's all the little things that end up being 'not quite exactly right' or 'not quite exactly what we were expecting' that trigger everyone's emotional reactions.

Accepting this reality, elite construction managers are remarkably good at navigating this ongoing battle with calm diligence

– not a battle against the project team, a battle against the highly imperfect process. They are capitalising on the unique application of Dr Angelou's wisdom by gracefully leading everyone through the fear storm of uncertainty, toward an ever-positive emotional state. They recognise that, at the end of every day, and every project, the way your client feels about the building experience you created for them, will literally trump the facts of whatever happened out there. The details will fade, but the feelings will last.

The seemingly dominant, highly technical, data-driven, science-like nature of the industry is largely an illusion. Remember, that part is essential but no longer enough. It's nowhere near the full story, and it's not the part that truly counts – in the end – when the final scores are tallied. Elite contractors have figured out that if feelings trump facts, then 'experience management' must trump construction management.

Here's the bottom line. Although it may be true that people often do business with people they like, or people they trust, those statements are cliché, a bit amateur and not at all specific enough to be helpful in our industry. So let me be very specific. In the built environment, one emotion will dominate the **decision-making** process – and that emotion is **fear.** It may often be disguised as frustration or anger, but deep down, in places where people emotionally hide because they are unable to articulate how they really feel, you will find most project owners desperately hoping for someone who can help them to be less afraid.

They literally need a hero. Picture a magic wand that wields the power to make everyone around you feel that somehow, some way, no matter what happens, we got this. Despite everything you thought you knew about what it means to be an excellent project manager or superintendent or any other critical position, the most successful people in our industry are the ones who possess that kind of positive emotional influence. Do they also have excellent construction management skills? Yes, obviously, those are critical and valuable. But their experience management skills will equal or exceed their construction management skills, and those are currently priceless.

Exploit this secret while you still can.

A project owner will hire and rehire the company who continuously makes them feel less afraid of whatever it is they are fearing in any given moment or situation. ***Figure out exactly what they are afraid of, work to alleviate that fear and help them to be less afraid while you are alleviating it.*** If you can do that, they will eventually forget the scary details and remember you as the one who helped them sleep at night, the one who convinced them that everything is going to be alright – and then made it so.

It's that simple.

And that incredibly hard.

But that's how you win.

ABOUT COTY FOURNIER

Coty Fournier is a prominent industry veteran with thirty years of complex design-build management and business development experience, as a corporate executive and entrepreneur in the built environment and related technology spaces. She leads with optimistic

---

1 **NOTE:** Some concepts in this chapter are inspired by and paraphrased from *Inside Commercial Construction's MVPs, Fournier*, Coty Leigh, Hunting House 2014-2024, with written permission from the author and publisher.

vision to consistently challenge the status quo, foster requisite change and inspire high-performance cultures. As a proven industry leader and motivational change agent, she is often tapped by construction companies and industry organisations for her exceptional training skills, growth strategies and executive leadership advisory. Known for her thought-provoking truth bombs, power talks and master classes at the intersection of talent and business development, Coty is leaving a well-marked trail along the fast track to success at the top of the construction management industry.

You can't teach this. You can't force someone to have it. You can't even have it on demand. Ryan Palmer shares a secret that is the undercurrent of winning in the game. This secret is akin to your overall lens that you can choose to look through, and you are the only one who can determine what lens you want to look through. Clouded or bright, you choose. This principle also lends itself to asking yourself bigger-picture questions, and when you allow yourself to determine your worldview, well, imagine how great the views can be ...

24

⨍TTITUDE OVER ⨍PTITUDE

BY RYAN PALMER

WHAT IS ONE THING YOU WOULD TELL A PERSON?

Choose attitude over aptitude.

WHY?

After nearly ten years on the tools within the building and construction industry, I have found the most valuable asset I have is my attitude. Reflecting on each stage of my career, from apprentice to tradesman and eventually to business manager, the one thing that has allowed me to succeed is having a positive attitude and being willing to accept that there's always more to learn. Aptitude can always be taught, but attitude is something that is innate that enables any individual to get the most out of situations put in front of them.

I have always had a passion for seeing young apprentices excel in their chosen trade. I have found, however, that in a world where they have endless information and answers at their fingertips, their confidence can take a hit when they don't have the technical knowledge. Fortunately for them, that is the whole point of an apprenticeship. In four years, you can learn all the technical skills you need to excel as a tradesperson. What can't be taught, though, is your work ethic. Asking questions, showing a willingness to learn and showing up with a smile on your face in the morning – these are all the things that will carry you further in your career than any technical skill ever will. And this same mentality can be transferred to every role, not just apprenticeships.

An apprenticeship is usually the first step into full-time work in the trade sector. It can be a rude shock to the system for most apprentices to suddenly be working long hours and having high expectations placed on them. After all, tradespeople aren't known for being subtle and will make it known when an apprentice isn't up to standard. But this is where attitude comes in. Even when you're struggling to meet those high expectations, a good attitude will serve you well. This is true no matter where you're at in your career, but in the early years of an apprenticeship it could be the difference between qualifying or not.

You must understand that maintaining a positive, open attitude isn't easy. It will take conscious effort. And there will be times when you slip out of a positive attitude. It certainly happened to me. When I came to the end of my apprenticeship, I fell into a bad loop. I wasn't happy with a few things at the company I worked for. Rather than do anything about it, I began to complain, and my productivity fell dramatically. It took a huge effort on my behalf to wake up every day, to do better and attempt to fix the situation I was in. I had to step back and change my attitude towards the issues I was facing, take ownership of the things I was doing to contribute to these issues and find what was in my control and what I could improve.

As I progressed in my career and transitioned into management roles, I found that maintaining my mentality of attitude over aptitude was just as critical now than ever before. I was once again learning new skills after having spent years honing my skills on the tools, and this was uncomfortable. Stepping into management is a big shift for most tradespeople. Suddenly, you're in charge of a team doing the job rather than doing the job yourself. Once again, this can be a shock, but maintaining the approach of attitude over aptitude can help you excel in the early stages of your career which is critical as you begin to climb the ladder. Faced with clients, my ability to stay positive and my willingness to ask questions were more relevant than ever – especially if I had no idea how I was going to accomplish a particular job.

Keeping an open and positive mindset will serve you well as you begin to learn the new skill set required for management. Being able to ask questions, ask for help or be honest about what you're capable of is a skill in itself. As issues arise – and issues always do – the attitude you put out into the work site will always reflect in the way your team handles these issues. Are you approachable? Can you communicate well? Do you seek advice from people that can help? Just like apprentices, so many new managers feel the need to have all the answers, but once again, an attitude of being willing to learn and ask questions will usually result in more collaboration and teamwork to help get the issue resolved.

This same principle and attitude of being willing to ask

questions and learn also applies before the work has even started.

I had someone reach out to me for a quote to install down lights in their kitchen, I could have easily looked at the job and told them what I believed was the best approach. I could have explained that I will install six downlights throughout the kitchen, to be wired from the existing light switch. I could have told the client we can do it in two weeks' time and how much it will cost. On paper, great service. I've told the client what, how, when and how much. However, I took the time to dig a little deeper with the questions. I asked about the job and why it was important the lighting was upgraded. The client told me that they had just moved in recently and their children sat at the kitchen table every night to do their homework while they cooked dinner, just like in their previous home. The lighting in the kitchen at the new home wasn't bright enough and the kids were getting headaches. This night-time routine was hugely important to the family as it gave them a chance to spend time together. If I can prove to the client that I have understood this, I will win that job even if I am more expensive or can't get there as soon as someone else can.

Attitude is everything. It can change the entire trajectory of your career like it did mine. Technical skills can be taught by someone else, but your attitude is yours to control, and I believe it can take you further than anything else in your career.

ABOUT RYAN PALMER

Ryan began his journey in the building and construction industry as an apprentice electrician in Adelaide, South Australia. During this time, he has worked his way through multiple different leading hand and management roles for nearly a decade.

With a passion for seeing young people succeed, Ryan has always enjoyed mentoring young apprentices as they enter the building and construction industry.

Ryan believes the building and construction industry is one that not only teaches valuable technical skills, but also life skills that extend beyond the work site.

Have you experienced real artforms? This could be a masterpiece, a building, car, shoe. Something that is made to such exquisiteness, so perfect, so moving? What was it? Think about what it would have taken that respective artist to produce and develop something to such a level of creation that others marvel at. Do you think this level of artistic endeavour is lost in what we consider an advanced and contemporary society? Phillip Spence shares a pivotal principle that underpins the possibility of the highest expression of our work, or better yet, our craft. You don't need to be a highly skilled craftsman, or even born with natural talents of any sort, but afforded to you here is a secret to imbibe excellence at whatever your hand touches.

25

HONOURING YOUR WORK

BY PHILLIP SPENCE

WHAT IS ONE THING YOU WOULD TELL A PERSON?
Honour your work.

WHY?
Many years ago, I had a profound experience that transformed my life. It all began when I received an invitation to leave my sales and marketing role in Australia and join my family business in the Caribbean. The business specialised in building finishes, paint manufacturing, waterproofing buildings and hydraulic engineering works. My father, who was owner and CEO, had been diagnosed with Alzheimer's disease and was no longer able to continue in his role. With no prior experience in this field, I was tasked with assuming his position. However, before doing so, I needed to gain knowledge and learn the necessary techniques. Therefore, I embarked on a six-month journey, travelling to six different locations around the world for intensive training.

Filled with eagerness, I arrived in the Caribbean, ready to establish myself as a respected authority in the business. Little did I know that this venture would turn into a role that would shape the next thirteen years of my working life. Throughout this transformative journey, I discovered the true meaning of honouring my work in the construction industry.

As the tropical sun bathed the vibrant landscapes, I witnessed a remarkable connection between honour and character. Honouring became more than a mere act; it evolved into a beacon of excellence, a reflection of the very essence of who I am as an individual and a professional. In a world often driven by self-interest and fleeting accomplishments, embracing honour as one of the highest standards an individual can bestow sets us apart. It ignites a fire within us, compelling us to approach our work with unwavering dedication and integrity. It becomes the driving force that propels us to go the extra mile, to surpass expectations and to create a lasting impact.

By honouring our work, we not only uplift ourselves but also inspire others to strive for greatness, fostering a culture of respect and admiration. This journey of honouring goes beyond a mere concept; it becomes a way of life, serving as an inspirational reminder of the immense power and beauty that lies within us when we choose to live true to our values, passions and aspirations. To foster pride and respect, our entire team focused on constantly learning about new processes, techniques and innovations, enhancing the expertise of all employees, including those with limited formal education. Despite their educational background, these individuals possessed remarkable skills in applying visually stunning and durable building finishes. Regular in-house and onsite training further boosted the confidence of the team, fuelling their motivation to pursue excellence.

One experience stands out, emphasising the importance of producing quality work; our waterproofing team who specialised in the application of high-density polyethylene lining were working on a reservoir for rainwater harvesting, designed to capture and contain rainwater runoff. Attention to detail and a commitment to quality were paramount, given the strict requirements and time lines enforced on the project. The team are our priority above all else and were tasked with lining a reservoir that would feed water to crops and cattle in an area near the slopes surrounding a mountainous region. By focusing on every aspect, from planning to execution, and maintaining adherence to high quality standards, we achieved exceptional results.

Of course, we faced challenges and pitfalls that hindered our progress such as being held up at gunpoint onsite by notorious gangland members and being asked for ransom money before the workers were allowed to continue their duties. In the boiling hot tropical midsummer where daily high temperatures are around thirty degrees Celsius and the humidity felt like it could be cut with a knife, this indeed had a negative effect on workers' emotions and behaviour. It's one thing to honour your work under perfect conditions, but when the cards aren't stacked in your favour, when obstacles test your resolve, that's when the true measure of honouring your work reveals itself.

To overcome these challenges and maintain a strong work ethic, effective time management was prioritised and shifts were put in place to reduce the possibility of heat exhaustion and dehydration. This involved providing copious amounts of fluids, allocating sufficient time for different tasks, allowing for thoroughness, attention to detail, setting realistic deadlines and openly communicating challenges which helped us manage time pressure effectively. We fostered a culture of open and transparent communication, regularly sharing progress, seeking feedback and addressing issues promptly. Building strong relationships and trust within the team helped workers stay focused and motivated even during tough times.

It's easy to cut corners, compromise integrity or succumb to the pressures of a hostile environment. Yet, it is precisely in those moments, when faced with adversity, that the importance of honouring our work shines brightest. It's about holding steadfast to our principles, even when it seems easier to take shortcuts. It's about finding the inner strength to maintain our commitment to excellence, despite the odds. When circumstances conspire against us, honour becomes the beacon that guides us through the darkest of times, reminding of the immense value that lies in upholding our craft with unwavering dedication.

So, let us remember that honouring our work goes beyond ideal conditions – it thrives amidst adversity, shaping integrity, resilience and true character. Leading construction companies have earned their reputation through consistent commitment to quality, professionalism and ethics, gaining respect and recognition. This highlights how honouring our work leads to remarkable achievements and enhances the construction industry's advancement and reputation.

ABOUT PHILLIP SPENCE

Phillip's passion for innovative solutions, combined with his collaborative approach and valuable insights earned him global industry recognition. His exceptional ability to identify opportunities and drive strategic growth coupled with his commitment to quality fuelled his entrepreneurial journey. Moreover, Phillip's thought leadership extends beyond business success as he prioritises building long-term relationships, leaving an indelible mark on the companies he serves. His expertise in analysing consumer behaviour and tailoring innovative solutions for specialised groups positions him as a trusted partner in achieving sustained growth and fostering enduring, impactful relationships.

The principle that hits the nail on the head. It takes an immense amount of courage in an individual to look at their life, despite having great successes, and say that they'd gotten a major part of it wrong and watch it all unfold in front of their eyes. Most people would call it quits after such experiences, fearing their place in the world and shutting off their future. Yet, Spiroula Stathakis shares her secret to ensuring that the comeback was stronger than the setback, and it wasn't done by conventional pathways of becoming. Actually, quite the opposite. The thing with truth is that it will be delivered to you whether you like it or not, so the path of least resistance is to awaken yourself to it, before you'll be made to realise …

26

THE UNLEARNING

BY SPIROULA STATHAKIS

WHAT IS ONE THING YOU WOULD TELL A PERSON?
Don't let your immediate environmental circumstances dictate your outcomes.

WHY?
Do you ever feel so debilitated by the fear of the unknown that you lose focus on the excitement of what could be?

I wasn't born into wealth, nor was I given my future on a silver platter, and I definitely was not surrounded by businesspeople. Quite the opposite, I was fired from my first job in the industry, and I even went through a divorce – all before thirty. I was, however, surrounded by love, but that love was still afraid. Nothing in my immediate environment supported the decisions I made in my life; I started my business with no safety net and no plan B. At one point in time, I was surrounded by so much toxicity that if I had allowed that energy to penetrate the rhetorical 'force field', I probably would have been sitting in a corner rocking somewhere. If I had looked for evidence in my then broken-down reality, my vision would have died a quick death.

Naturally as human beings, we are conditioned through various scenarios we experience in our environment, which could stem back to our childhood. We're told to be safe, 'don't do this', 'don't touch that' or 'you'll hurt yourself'. These fears are unknowingly drummed into our subconscious mind by our family, our friends and our colleagues as a way of projecting their own fears and limitations onto you because they themselves can't fathom overcoming their limitations. We try our hardest to resist at times and carve our own paths, only to have those same, small-minded people pull us back into their limited realities. What would happen if we CHOSE to say no? What if we chose to create a rhetorical force field around us that repelled the negativity and constraints of others? As William James put it, 'When you have to make a choice, and don't make it, that in itself is a choice.' Ask yourself, *Who's reality am I living in exactly?*

Naturally, we revert to our comfort zones when life gets tough and make statements to support that, whether it be in our personal or professional lives. We go through a divorce, 'There's no point dating, no-one wants me.' We lose our job, 'I should settle for the first thing that comes along instead of following my passion.' We create our narrative based on our own inner voice, that has been trained and conditioned to save us from perceived 'danger'. However, that same reaction of 'fight or flight' was what cavemen used to run from a lion. The same feedback we continue to have as humans is in direct response to an outdated and primitive way of being. We no longer need to run for our lives or hunt and gather our food, so why is our fight or flight response still so strong? Your mind thinks you're in constant danger, but have you really looked at your environment? Because the evolution of the human brain's survival mechanism hasn't advanced to align with the freedoms we have in this current world.

Our parents, grandparents and so on were all taught the same basic survival principles which greatly revolves around fear, which is then taught to every generation to follow, until someone breaks that pattern and decides they want more for themselves and that the limiting beliefs they've been taught is merely a projection of fear and not 'truth'. Think about it – you've confined yourself to situations created hundreds of years ago …

Truth is personal. It's our perception of self, our confidence levels and our capabilities. Even that, at times, can let us down. Some might believe you are merely the manifestation of your immediate environment and that your reality and your future is dictated by opportunities that are given to you. It can't be further from the truth, well at least, my truth. Success and happiness IS my birthright – it's yours too.

I chose from an early age that, despite the fears and resistance from my environment and that dreaded inner voice, I was going to make my vision, my life, my goals work. I made a promise that I was going to find the silver lining in every scenario that took place in my life.

It's not about what happens to you, but how you respond to it that determines the character of a person.

I was going to fight for the future I wanted, and I know I deserve, and I was going to break the multigenerational conditioning I had been brought up believing as truth. I am a child of migrant parents, incredibly hardworking, from Greece with very little and made a life for themselves in Australia strongly based around their own sense of resilience and wonder. Their idea of success was to one day own their home, have their children and maybe, if they're lucky, have an investment property. It was the 'Australian dream'.

Thankfully, they did that, and it taught me resilience and strength. It also taught me the importance of hard work whilst instilling in me a great sense of faith. Not necessarily in the religious sense, but faith that things will work out, no matter what. I hold onto that faith for dear life, and it is my guiding star through every decision I have made to date, no matter how big or small. What else is there to lean on to break away from your current environment? From deciding to take on projects that I had no idea I could do, deciding to end my marriage in search of a life I knew I deserved, to deciding to start a business and give it everything I had, I leant on faith. In the words of Richard Branson, 'If somebody offers you an amazing opportunity but you are not sure you can do it, say yes – then learn how to do it later!' A quote that has resonated with me for years, the reason why I was able to work on some of the most incredible projects and make life-changing decisions (with no plan B).

Will you choose to expand your mind and see new horizons, despite your environment and your current circumstances, or will you choose to retract into a scarcity mindset? Jim Rohn once stated that, 'You're the average of the five people you spend the most time with,' there is so much truth in this statement, which is why you should strive to find your people, however, there will be occasions where your immediate environment won't allow you to cut ties with the very energy that might be dimming your glow. In those instances, you must find the resilience and strength within yourself. You must hold onto your dream and vision with both hands and not let go. Find ways by delving deeper into your inner consciousness and find your 'why'. Naturally, your force field will grow, and your belief of self will surpass the negativity you may be surrounded with.

Remember that there is no such thing as the perfect time, there is only now.

ABOUT SPIRUOLA STATHAKIS

Spiroula's portfolio extends to national and pioneer levels, having designed showrooms for some of the largest companies across the country, working on Australia's first co-living space and being part of the incredible team at Sydney's Crown Casino amongst many others. Winning design awards, Australian Women's Business finalist, Business NSW Outstanding Business Leader Finalist, Business Elite's '40 under 40', working within the media, ambassadorships, podcasts, coaching, judging and keynote presentations, has secured her position within the industry as an expert in her own right with a cornucopia of experience which she endeavours to expand on through her business' FOS Collective and The Elite Interior Design Academy. As an ambitious individual who wants to continue making waves in the design industry and ensure the next generation is equipped with the tools to succeed, Spiroula places great importance on continued growth and evolution in order to change the design landscape as we know it.

Is life a game of things just falling into place, or do you control the chain of events that ensue? Is our path premeditated or more a choose-your-own-adventure game? And isn't retrospect a great teacher and bringer of wisdom? Yet, to get to a point of experiential wisdom, not just armchair philosophy, you need to get out there, and with what you have, where you are and what you know, give it your best and your most. Which is what Matt DiBara does, allowing his business and life to expand in ways that wouldn't have been possible if he simply stayed in one place. Think of this best-kept secret like a video game. The more that you move and run forward, up and down, over and under, the game continues to load, and you go to another level, and another level ... So, how do you want to play the game? Let's try Matt's principle on for size and see how you can really win at any level ...

27

THE DOMINO EFFECT

BY MATT DIBARA

WHAT IS ONE THING YOU WOULD TELL A PERSON?
Understand the importance of the *domino effect* in your life.

WHY?
Have you ever gotten to a point in your life and stopped to take a moment to consider the purposeful, yet sometimes random, chain of events that got you to where you are today?

Surely, you've marvelled at a moment in time, thinking if you hadn't trusted your internal guidance to take a right, instead of left, how different life could have been for you?

Or have you taken a moment to trace back your trajectory to a thought, an event, and then seen how everything just worked out from there?

And simply sat there and thought, *If it wasn't for … I wouldn't be here …*

When you take a moment to marvel at the domino effect in

your life, you truly come to realise the importance of it, and why setting the first domino in motion is critical to a massive chain reaction for yourself.

I've often been asked about my journey, the successes, the challenges and what has led me to the point I am at today. It's easy to attribute our achievements to a single brilliant idea or a defining moment, but in reality, it's the subtle interplay of countless decisions, actions and circumstances that has shaped my path. This is what I call the domino effect.

My journey wasn't easy. I can fill pages talking about the challenges I have faced in my life, from taking over a family business to almost losing everything a few years later. But I do not look at these challenges as hurdles, instead, I consider them moments that pushed me to work harder and always have an impact on how the next domino will move or fall into place. When you take a macro perspective on what is playing out in your life and know that it's part of a larger chain of events, you will find more purpose in navigating through said hurdles as they eventuate for you.

Let's rewind fifteen years, back to a time when I was just a young kid, eager to learn and help my dad in managing our family business. Our family has a rich history in construction, stemming from my grandparents, Matteo and Michael, who immigrated to the US from Italy in the early 1900s. They built their homes showcasing their craftsmanship. Neighbours admired their work and began requesting their assistance, which was the spark that ignited our family masonry business. This, to me, is a prime example of the domino effect – a series of decisions and actions that set the course for our family's legacy.

From my early teenage days, I knew I wanted to be a part of our family business. While most kids my age were busy playing sports, I was right there with my dad, sorting rocks for stone walls and digging holes for foundations at our masonry company. I didn't mind coming home dirty because it symbolised my commitment to our craft. Despite the judgemental eyes and negative opinions, I was resolute in following my dreams. This period was marked by an essential domino, the *Dirty Jobs* TV show hosted by Mike Rowe, which celebrated skilled trades and reinforced the value of such careers.

Consider how some of the earlier dominoes in your life have set off a chain reaction, hopefully for the better in your life. What opportunities do you see coming into your life as a result of the actions today? That TV show opportunity wasn't a random experience, it was already in motion, long before I even fathomed it a possibility, but cemented (pun intended) what would come next.

My journey continued as I enrolled in the masonry program at Montachusett Regional Vocational Technical High School in Massachusetts and joined SkillsUSA, a requirement for competing. I vividly recall my first competition, where I placed third in my school in the bricklaying competition. This was another domino as it pushed me into a world of competition, one I didn't want to be a part of but one that helped me find greater success in life. I encourage you to think about the domino effect also as not being a linear one, but one that branches off into multiple variables that, again, create even more opportunity and open more doors in your life.

This realisation fuelled my passion and led me to participate in more competitions, ultimately achieving significant victories.

I don't share this for the sake of it, but to highlight that the domino effect enabled me to tap into more hunger and drive to continue excelling and upskilling in my craft. This is another domino because this win helped me move in the right direction and the tools I won at the national competition stayed with me. In fact, these tools were the last items I placed in my car before embarking on a journey to California to relocate our family masonry business. These tools became symbols of my progress and contributed to my success in a new state.

One domino kept falling after another. When you start seeing your trajectory as a bigger picture and there's no such thing as an isolated event or reaction, you will be able to move more purposefully, intently and consciously, and tapping into more faith that you are going exactly where you need to. The domino effect in your life, when trusted, will only lead you to continuously grander outcomes that demand more from you, to achieve more.

From the relocation, I saw the opportunity to set up another business, moving from managing a single company to owning multiple businesses, including The Contractor Consultants, which aids construction companies in hiring and retaining talent and establishing a foothold in the industry. From that, I continue to do many more things – speaking, connecting, shows and more. The importance of the domino effect in my life has shown me the possibilities of constantly opening up new horizons, because I fundamentally trust the process, and that all events, no matter how macro or micro they are, are leading me to where I need to be. It's not necessarily destiny, but it is living with more conscious intent, which you too can introduce into your life when you decide to move with more faith, than fear, and understand the intricate purpose and relationship within all things that happen in your life.

I've witnessed firsthand how even the smallest choices and opportunities can trigger a chain reaction. When I reflect on my past, I see how saying 'yes' to one project led to valuable connections, how persevering through tough times built resilience and how learning from failures ultimately paved the way for success. One thing leading to another, so perfectly, in retrospect.

The domino effect is a potent concept, reminding us that our lives are a series of interconnected moments, each influencing the next. It's not solely about the significant leaps; it's about the daily decisions, the consistent efforts and the ability to adapt and learn from each experience. Can you make a seemingly small but significant decision for yourself today? Just see what it could set into motion for you …

The domino effect has taught me that even in the face of challenges, setbacks or uncertainty, I can trust that my efforts will ultimately have a positive impact on my entrepreneurial journey. It's important that you use this concept to remain connected to your bigger picture and not let one piece alone dictate the whole game for you.

Stay mindful of the interconnectedness of your experiences and recognise that your perseverance and dedication will set in motion a chain reaction of success that you may not fully appreciate until you look back and see how the dominos have fallen in your favour.

ABOUT MATT DIBARA

Matt DiBara: Championing tradition, empowering futures.

Matt DiBara, a well-known figure of the skilled trades and entrepreneurship, stands as a testament to the enduring legacy of DiBara Masonry. As a fourth-generation owner, Matt's commitment to craftsmanship and his family's heritage runs deep within his story.

His passion traces back to high school, where his interest for the trades started during his journey through SkillsUSA. Starting his hands-on work at just nine years old, Matt incorporated the essence of pride in his craft, honing his skills through dedication and persistence.

Today, he stands as an entrepreneurial success, his achievements reflecting a narrative of resilience and determination. By the age of twenty-seven, he was already contributing to the construction of awe-inspiring celebrity homes. But what really sets him apart is how he's always championing the trades and firmly backing aspiring entrepreneurs.

A revered speaker, Matt's inspirational presence resonates far beyond his endeavours. Speaking to over fifteen thousand high school students at SkillsUSA, his journey was featured in SkillsUSA Champions. Co-founding The Contractor Consultants, he's created the first-ever sixty-three-module contractor hiring course and partnered with industry giants like ZipRecruiter and Indeed.

Matt's impact isn't confined to speeches, his presence is felt at prestigious industry events such as RoofCon and World of Concrete, earning notable features in ACHR News and Pro Remodeler. Recently, gracing Tarek El Moussa's The Flipping Summit, he shared his expertise and infectious passion, inspiring countless aspiring tradespeople and entrepreneurs alike.

How predictable is the human mind? Do you think it's impossible to predict human behaviour? It's actually more predictable and controllable than you think, or better said, would like to think. The human mind is akin to a computer program, which can be commanded in any which way imaginable. Now, this can be and has been used for nefarious reasons, but it can also be used for the collective betterment, especially when it comes to site safety. I found the results of Ray Ramsay on megaprojects to be astounding, as he realised the secret that underpins performance and behaviour. If you want to attain any influential advantage in whatever you do, there's a principle to doing it ...

28

Wired for Safety: Psychology and Behaviour in Metro Construction Projects

BY RAY RAMSAY

What is one thing you would tell a person?

People take the path of least resistance. The key to understanding why is through human behavioural patterns.

Why?

The construction of a metro system is an immense undertaking that demands unwavering attention to safety. Possessing a comprehensive and profound understanding of human behaviour becomes pivotal in ensuring the safety of workers and the public during the ongoing metro construction works at Central station, regardless of the project's complexity.

The construction work at Central has been described as, 'Performing open heart surgery on a patient that is conscious!' To say that managing risk and safety elements of these works was a challenge was an understatement.

When you are dealing with the public and Sydney Trains staff, there are over 700,000 people utilising Central station daily, so, there is always a risk or hazard that needs to be addressed, and that's during the standard operations of the station. Include the eight-hundred-plus construction team, working twenty-four-hour shifts, that's a lot of people. Any of which could have a safety incident.

Let's not forget that Central station used to be a cemetery, so there was a fair bit of archaeological work – the removal of crypts and human remains. There were plenty of hazardous materials that were required to be safely removed, thousands of tonnes of soil, solely for laying of 100km of optic fibre.

Once the footprint of the construction area was available and the demolition had been completed, the works moved sub-terranean. All the standard environmental hazards were at the forefront. Noise, dust and vibration. Add to the mix the numerous complaints from staff about the perceived environmental hazards and ongoing risk assessments became the norm. Then add in COVID-19 protocols, drug and alcohol testing, and fatigue management, the list is quite endless.

Numerous areas of the station required to be boarded off, and new passenger walkways were constructed just to move customers and staff around the station. Staff had to be briefed on the construction activities and schedule, and my job was to ensure there was no interruption to rail operations and maintenance.

My priority was to ensure the safety of customers and all transport staff in the station precinct. Remember, this was happening above ground in live environments and underground.

Even though this was a five-year project, the construction work needed to be completed on schedule, but the core objective was to ensure there was no disruption to the rail operations and maintenance and minimal impact to customers and staff.

In the five years of construction activities in and around Central station, *there were no notable safety incidents that resulted in any serious injury to staff or the public.* Sit with the magnitude of that for a moment.

Now, implementing safety and risk systems is a stock standard part of construction methodology. My primary objective was to ensure there were no safety incidents and everyone at Central went home safe. It would seem to be a given that with such a project as Central, all would uphold the highest of standards, but human nature is to do the bare minimum and see how they can get away with it.

One of the keys to achieving this outstanding result on a megaproject was to understand how people behave the way they do. Why do people take shortcuts? Are they encouraged to do so? Why would they put the safety of themselves or their workmates at risk? To the logical mind, that's crazy. Yet, despite what most think, people do not act logically, but of deeply wired patterns of behaviour. My task was to create new habits and change the existing wired patterns.

What seems logical to one, isn't always so to another. By understanding human behaviour, I was able to utilise our secret weapon for risk and safety culture implementation: subliminal neurolinguistic programming. Planting messages subconsciously to create new safety habits.

99.9% of the teams had no idea it was implemented. This is using a number of key phrases in implementing a safety message into each individual via the communications channel and having them repeat it daily. Every day. These messages played on the subconscious emotions of each individual; we stressed in the messaging, 'There someone waiting for you at home. Make sure you don't disappoint them!'

Using psychology to understand how people operate and how they will act – this is the secret. Planting subliminal messages and consistently advising on the need to be safe created long-term behavioural shifts. Safety is one of the primal cognitive initiatives hardcoded into all our brains from an early age. Most individuals will retain seven pieces of information at any given time. Ensuring that a safety message was number one on that information flow was a key function of the behavioural changes that were imprinted in their conscious and subconscious memory.

Contrary to popular belief, simply repeating a message doesn't create the desired outcome. What matters is how is the message delivered in a way that meets the programming of the receiver.

If the message is communicated effectively, consistently and demanded by the project owners, the message will be imprinted on people's minds. The safety messages formed part of every team's ethos. Eventually, safety became a habit, rather than a chore. Management was of their primary thoughts on safety, not their behaviours. Having posters with the key safety messages planted in all the critical work areas, that no-one could miss, is a component of how they are instilled in people's subconscious.

Having them on the back of toilet doors was a real inspiration. Who would have thought that would work on a megaproject?

Those who thought they didn't need reminders and caused minor incidents were shown the door. One thing that people forget about is safety incidents cost the project time and money.

It set the tone and showed that people had to be responsible. It also implanted another subliminal message – 'Conform or leave!'

Another little message was linked to the fact there were surveillance officers who would report breaches. Construction staff knew if they were caught doing the wrong thing, it would be reported. I had to shut down construction on a couple of occasions to initiate a safety stop.

I have to admit, this is not unusual; psychological profiling has been used in other industries for years. I was just amazed by how using NLP techniques worked as well as it did to convey such fundamental messages and yield desired safety metrics.

If you want to ensure a robust and sound risk and safety culture for a construction project, consider how behavioural psychology works in implementation, and embed some NLP messaging into the communications.

The final finish of a megaproject is often used to judge its success. However, it's important to remember that people are the key factor in any project's success. Ensuring that workers go home safe every day is the most important measure of a project's success.

ABOUT RAY RAMSAY

Ray Ramsay is an experienced risk professional with over thirty years of experience in risk and safety management. He has worked in various environments including financial services, major corporations and government agencies. Ray has an MBA and qualifications in risk, safety and human factors, as well as psychology and kinetics. He is a strategic thinker who can work with all levels of management to deliver practical solutions that support decision-makers with quality information.

Ray has experience in designing, implementing and continually improving risk frameworks, program risk management, safety risk assurance, audit, fraud and corruption. He has also worked as a fraud investigator and has many years of experience evaluating the way people behave.

It's that old adage — risk vs. reward, benefit vs. cost, but how much is one holding back the other, and what do you think this means for our collective progress? Pooja Mahajan brings to surface a key consideration of a principle that impacts us all, personally and professionally.

29

BALANCING ACTS: NAVIGATING RISK-AVERSE APPROACHES AND INNOVATION WITHIN THE CONSTRUCTION INDUSTRY

BY POOJA MAHAJAN

The construction industry has historically exhibited a pronounced inclination towards risk aversion. Faced with substantial financial investments and stringent safety regulations, stakeholders in this field tend to approach projects cautiously, emphasising predictability and stability. The inherent complexity of construction projects, coupled with the potential for unforeseen challenges, has contributed to a prevailing culture of risk mitigation.

At the forefront of risk aversion in construction lies safety – not only for the workers navigating construction sites but also for the broader public utilising the resulting infrastructure. A robust risk-averse strategy is indispensable for systematically identifying and proactively addressing potential hazards. Ensuring safety for workers and the public necessitates a proactive approach that extends beyond mere compliance with safety regulations to a comprehensive risk management ethos.

The substantial capital involved in construction projects amplifies the significance of financial prudence. Contractual obligations, penalties for delays and the looming spectre of cost overruns underscore the economic risks inherent in these endeavours. A risk-averse approach is not only a matter of operational prudence but becomes a strategic imperative for safeguarding long-term financial viability.

The uniqueness of each construction site further accentuates the need for a customised risk-averse approach. For example, constructing a high-rise building in a seismic zone demands considerations beyond the standard project parameters. A site-specific risk aversion approach may involve specialised engineering designs, stringent quality control measures and onsite safety protocols tailored to the specific challenges presented by the seismic context. However robust the fortress of risk aversion may be, it prompts a pertinent question: How does one balance this cautious approach with the imperative for innovation? The construction industry, like any other, is not immune to the winds of change, and embracing innovation becomes a testament to resilience. The challenge lies not in forsaking the tried and tested but in seamlessly integrating the novel into established practices. Innovation in construction can take various forms – novel materials, cutting-edge methodologies or transformative technologies. However, the challenge lies in introducing these innovations without compromising the industry's hard-earned risk-averse ethos. In recent times, the shift to a risk-sharing model is evident in approaches like design-build. In a design-build scenario, a single entity is responsible for both the design and construction phases, fostering collaboration and shared accountability among stakeholders.

Despite this positive shift, challenges persist, particularly regarding the industry's overall resistance to embracing novel ideas. To address this, strategic pilot projects can be implemented, enabling stakeholders to test innovative materials or methodologies on a smaller scale before full-scale integration, as illustrated by the example of incorporating eco-friendly building materials in a designated section of a construction project. Strategic pilot projects enable stakeholders to test innovations on a manageable scale, providing insights into real-world implications, both positive and negative. Consider a scenario where a construction project contemplates incorporating a new, eco-friendly building material with purported cost savings. Instead of implementing this material across the entire project, a strategic pilot project would designate a specific section for its application, allowing for a meticulous evaluation of its performance and impact.

To catalyse innovation within organisations involves cultivating a startup culture. By adopting agile methodologies and a design thinking approach to address common infrastructure problems and fostering a mindset shift through targeted training, organisations can initiate a transformative journey. Clear metrics to gauge success, along with a structured approach to assess impact, provide a foundation for this process. As successes accumulate, organisations can gradually expand initiatives, seamlessly integrating innovation into their fabric. This deliberate and incremental approach enables organisations to embrace innovation, fostering a dynamic and forward-thinking culture.

In the current landscape of construction, sensorisation is becoming ubiquitous, generating a vast amount of valuable data in both small- and large-scale implementations. This data, harvested from sensors monitoring structural health, environmental conditions and worker activities, serves as a goldmine for the industry, providing unprecedented insights and paving the way for transformative innovations.

Consider a scenario where construction sites are already equipped with an extensive network of sensors. These sensors enable real-time data analytics for proactive interventions. For instance, in urban planning, imagine a city with sensors monitoring traffic flow, air quality and energy consumption. The real-time data harvested from these sensors becomes a vital resource for predictive analytics, allowing city officials to optimise traffic management, address pollution concerns and enhance energy efficiency. This data-driven approach not only improves urban living but also acts as a catalyst for expanding sensorisation within the urban environment.

The insights gleaned from existing sensor networks can inform decisions on expanding and refining the infrastructure of data collection. This iterative process sets the stage for incorporating advanced technologies like machine learning (ML) and artificial intelligence (AI), digital twins and building information modelling (BIM).

The construction industry finds itself at a perpetual juncture, caught between the security of a risk-averse approach driven by high stakes and the imperative to innovate and progress. It's evident that the industry cannot abruptly embrace extensive risks solely for the sake of innovation. Instead, a careful and deliberate balance remains the key to forging a different future. This dynamic tension between caution and innovation underscores the industry's challenge and opportunity: to continue building a future that blends the tried and tested with the novel and progressive. The key lies in acknowledging that innovation and risk aversion are not mutually exclusive but rather complementary aspects of a dynamic industry.

ABOUT POOJA MAHAJAN

Pooja Mahajan is a dynamic professional whose career has evolved from civil engineering to product management within the AEC industry. With over a decade of experience in project engineering and management, her expertise lies in wastewater treatment, environmental compliance, and stormwater management. This technical foundation has been instrumental as she transitioned to developing technology products. Currently, as a product manager, Pooja applies her engineering insights to innovate SaaS products focused on complex environmental challenges, such as predicting landslide and flood risks. She plays a crucial role in guiding the research, development, and refinement of new and existing software features, making significant contributions to developing cutting-edge solutions tailored for the AEC sector.

Nikola Tesla, inventor, electrical engineer, mechanical engineer and futurist said, 'If you want to find the secrets of the universe, think in terms of energy, frequency and vibration.' Now, consider that you are the universe, and there you have the greatest secret for hacking this life. You've been thinking about the model incorrectly, assuming that if you just work harder, do more hours, smash out more emails, that you'll achieve more. You're not thinking on the right plane on the root of the science of achievement. Brenda Denbesten has realised that the never-ending to-do list can't be achieved through finite resources. Yet, there is something which is infinite within you to underpin any level of achievement you want to go for ...

30

THE HIGHLY UNDERRATED CURRENCY

BY BRENDA DENBESTEN

WHAT IS ONE THING YOU WOULD TELL A PERSON?

Manage your energy, and you manage the quality and output of your life.

WHY?

People always ask me how I always find a way to get things done. Because in today's world everyone wants to get the outcome without going through the process. People are seeking microwave solutions to everything, whether that is career promotions, profitable side hustles or the coveted summer body.

The underlying foundation to getting things done comes down to energy management. This isn't a topic exclusive to power companies or operational managers and CEOs. Energy is the highest form of currency that everyone on this earth possesses. However, the awareness of that currency varies across the board. Energy can be expressed through time, through emotions, through your reactions. When you have low energy, your zest for life diminishes, and often it's your personal life that suffers. Many are in the habit of giving to work first, going above and beyond, saying yes to all the things, then feeling drained once they walk through the door. Minimal energy left for their loved ones, children and most importantly for themselves.

It would be easy for me to identify as a victim. Let me share the laundry list as to why:

- I am a FIFO wife – my husband works in a different state on a week-on, week-off roster.
- I have two children, who I must solo parent when my husband is away.
- I work five days a week managing two factories in two different states.
- I work in a male-dominated industry as a woman of multiple intersectional ties.
- I run a business where I help women in male-dominated industries step up, speak up and stand out to create a life they love.
- I also volunteer for organisations that support missions I resonate with.
- I write books, manage my YouTube channel and am a TEDx speaker finalist (at the time of writing).

All these things require a lot of mental, physical and

emotional currency to regulate and manage. So, the common question I receive when I tell people all the things I am juggling is, 'How do you handle all the things?' And the way I do this is through my energy. This critical resource isn't visible to the naked eye, but like electricity, it powers everything it is connected to. If you want to get more out of life, manage your energy.

Everybody likes to talk about boundaries where you stay firm and draw the line, but in reality, what you are doing with boundaries is protecting your energy so you can invest it in the things that will multiply productively. It's our job to hold and enforce the boundaries we set, as others simply follow our lead.

Choose to give your energy to things that replenish your energy. When you invest your energy unreciprocated then you feel drained. The common term for this is energy vampires ...

Just like weeds, when given free reign they will multiply. Ask yourself these questions when you find yourself in a slump, feeling burnt-out or 'without enough time' for things:

- Are you paying attention to your energy?
- Who are you giving your energy away to?
- What is the return on investment for your energy?

Another currency of energy is through other people's time and energy. Asking for help and support is a way to leverage energy so you are not doing it all yourself. This is very evident as a busy working parent, as I leverage the energy of child cares, the in-laws, my partner, my peers and my friends.

This is how I can keep going when everything around me is

turbulent. Where your focus goes, energy flows. When you feel stuck, or the environment in your workplace is toxic, I always advise my peers and clients to reassess. What is important to them? What do they value? Because at the end of the day you want to spend your days surrounded by situations and people who celebrate, appreciate and reciprocate your energy.

Other ways you can replenish your energy include getting enough sleep, soaking in the sunshine and fresh air, moving your body through exercise or a brisk walk, drinking lots of water and healthy food, following your passions and what lights you up, making peace your priority and choosing to be open and curious about life.

Think of your energy like a rechargeable battery. You decide who plugs into you and who you are transferring it to. In the heat of the moment, whether it be a conversation at work or home you could choose to blow up, shout and blame others for poor results or outcomes. This decision is like going from zero to sixty kilometres an hour very quickly – results in energy expulsion and can leave you feeling empty at the end of a long ten- or twelve-hour shift. Instead of making the situations mean something about you, ride the emotional wave and respond when you are back in a neutral space. This energy use is like changing from gear three to four in comparison with a blow up. Notice when you are in situations that give and take from your energy.

You are the guardian of your energy. If you wish to live a life that you enjoy and achieve more of your goals than the average person, the underlying secret is to manage your energy.

ABOUT BRENDA DENBESTEN

As a chemical engineer with over fifteen years' experience in the mining, manufacturing and construction industries, Brenda Denbesten is an advocate and driver for change.

She is a two-time Women in Industry award finalist for 'Excellence in Engineering' and 'Excellence in Manufacturing' categories and bestselling co-author of The FIFO Wives' Tales.

Brenda provides speaking, mentoring and coaching services for driven female engineers so they can get in the driver's seat, gain clarity on their unique strengths and the confidence to get ahead in traditional and male-dominated fields.

And then there is the question which has served as my ongoing catalyst for transformation, remaining insatiable with the answer, seeking to understand what lays in the peripheries of self. It's the infinite world that lays within us that captivates and grabs, versus the ordinary reality experienced by our five senses. There's one simple question, that if each individual pursues with courage and curiosity can elevate the individual and collective consciousness, and the one thing that finally I would love to share with you to close out the foray of secrets ...

31

THE GREATEST QUESTION

BY ELINOR MOSHE

WHAT IS ONE THING YOU WOULD TELL A PERSON?

The most important path you can be on is to discover who you are.

WHY?

If you seek to understand yourself, you will understand the universe. If you seek to understand the universe, you will understand yourself. When was the last time you wondered in your vastness, greatness, the magic of your creation? When was the last time you expressed deep and genuine curiosity for *all* that you are and why are you the way you are? The shallowed exploration of self in the majority of society is seen in the hollowed-out, blank expressions, robotic, autopilot, conformity-minded behaviours that most are regretfully surrounded by and interact with daily. Does it make sense to you that majority of the industry have similar passions, tastes, lifestyles, ambitions – make it make sense.

To me, *Who am I?* is the ultimate question, which has often sent me down pathways of discovery, most of which offered no possibility of return to who I once was. Nor was there desire to return there. Think of it as wearing clothing from five years ago, it's simply not you anymore. When posed with that question, majority will relay their job title, country of birth, religion, sexual orientation, industry, archive of degrees and even their name (but are you your name?). This is the composite of one's external identity, which has nothing to do with who you really are. They're mere factors that we've attached to our existing as a functional member of society. I've stumped many in mentoring sessions when asking them to introduce themselves without reference to externalities. External identities are again not too dissimilar to outfits – they're simply not you.

However, the inner self is a wonderland of realisations that mask and eclipse any ego attachment to an external factor of who you think you are. Do you think that you came into this world with no unique essence and you needed a degree to identify yourself with? Is the creator that stupid? To not explore who you are is to laugh and mock the creator, and say that man and his manmade systems need to tell me who I am, not the supreme, infinite intelligence of which we are born. Before you even questioned if you had a purpose, it was coded into you. The question is, will you find it?

Your internal identity is your original alchemy, the blueprint that was used when your componentry of self was put together. Like the instruction manual when you buy flat-pack furniture. We all have that, and we also have been given the tools to read this blueprint, assemble us and then present it so purposefully to the world. Your inner essence is more than your purpose. It's what truly makes you come alive, it's your natural disposition outside of conditioning, it's your natural gravitation, the unique gifts already within you, it's your strongest tendencies and affiliations that are you, without anyone having told you that it's you. And more.

Fine, you may say, *how do I find this out?* Contrary to popular belief, a five-minute inquiry into self will reveal nothing. This question has no end. Nor should you be satisfied with doing a basic DISC assessment, asking yourself two questions and professing that you are your authentic self. Yet, to enquire within requires time. And what do professionals love professing they have nothing of? Time. Enquiry into self is a non-linear path. Clarity doesn't come in an instance, which negates the dominant left-brained society who only see black-and-white answers. For most people, if they can't see it, they can't believe it. Most people are also not surrounded by those who engage in deep self-exploration, so their mediocrity and surface-level thinking is validated. Whilst the list of reasons why people don't discover themselves is endless, I will mention ego in conclusion. If you think you already know it all, what more could there possibly be to know? (Wrong.) Yet, that is the trick, the illusion that you're highly likely currently under – thinking that you are really you, when you've never really been you.

Because I kept on asking myself this question and remained convicted and never satisfied on the path, knowing there is more depth available, I have today, as I write, reached a point of dissolution, disconnection and realignment of who I thought I was, versus who I really am. I know that statement will remain as pertinent to me now as it will in years to come. Once the questioning within yourself starts, it doesn't stop.

Underneath (intergenerational) trauma bonds, cultural conditioning, educational paradigms, corporate restrictions and parental domestication lies a version of you that has unlikely seen the light of day for decades. Entertain that notion even for a minute, considering that right now, you are not all of who you can be. Do you not owe it to yourself to give yourself the greatest revelation of all? Not every part of you that resides within you is online at this moment in time. It's a fallacy to assert that it is. You haven't experienced all of you, and I'm not talking about the achievements and possibilities that await you in the external world.

The hardest thing for many to do, myself included when I started this journey, is commit identity suicide. To cause the ego death through unattachment so that I can be rebirthed. If that sounds foreign to you, good. It means there's so much more for you to explore. In the exploration of who you are will be found the releasing of who you are not, and to get what you truly desire, in your hearts of hearts, you'll be shown the path to your own unravelling. There, you'll likely meet yourself for the first time.

Whilst I strongly desire to pen more on this, I will leave you with one simple question: *Who are you?*

ABOUT ELINOR MOSHE

Elinor Moshe is an ambitious and driven thought leader, mentor, bestselling author, award-winning podcast host and businesswoman disrupting the construction industry. She's the founder of The Construction Coach, Australia's first construction coach constructing exceptional, excellent and exemplary people behind the projects. She is the recipient of the 'Best Construction Training Company 2022 – Australia' by **Build** *magazine.*

Her third book, Young Gun, *was awarded 'Best in Education' at the Author's Book Expo plus two additional awards. She is also the bestselling author of* Leadership in Construction *and* Constructing Your Career. *Elinor Moshe has been featured in* **Medium, Entrepreneur Asia Pacific** *and* **Yahoo! Finance** *for her career, leadership and business acumen and over fifty global podcasts. She is also the two-time award-winning podcast host of* **Constructing You** *where she interviews exemplary leaders, industry titans and young guns.*

CONCLUSION

Now it's your turn.

What is one thing you would tell a person?

Take a photo of the book, or you reading the book, and share your own defining principle on social media. Why? Because society could use a massive intellectual upgrade, and I encourage voices of truth and wisdom to *share*. What's your secret? What have you been vying to scream from the rooftops? Tell us. Did any chapter resonate with you in particular? You can also share your thoughts in continuity, so the online space is filled with conversations of distinct intellect, instead of pseudo-motivation, tactics and *another hack*. If a particular principle has stood out to you, I encourage you to connect with the co-author on LinkedIn and let them know.

As you conclude your foray into this anthology, allow yourself to come back to the pages when you feel lost, stuck or conflicted in your path. Remember, every co-author here has given you a golden set of keys to win. You can even pick up the book when you are stuck, ask the question, flick through the pages and intuitively stop. The answer that you need could be right there.

I hope that your journey into discovery doesn't end here, and that you continue to bring more depth, questioning, meaning and valuable exchange in your conversations. So many conversations are mechanical, perfunctory and lack an open and honest exchange without personal attack. Where can you challenge convention, an idea or otherwise, to bring in higher order thinking?

The more you seek to align your thinking with truth, wisdom and higher values, shall you always come out on top. Be humble enough and hungry enough to accept that the one-dimensional world view of most is not all that there can be, it's simply impossible.

Many desire for the industry to change – they'll even go to the extent of sticking a motivational poster on the wall to show that. But few will do what it really takes to elicit any sort of macro-level change, and that is themselves.

You may have got to this point only to identify that the secrets aren't really secrets. They've been in reach to you all along, but there's one thing left to do: act.

Wherever this book may find you in your journey in the industry, I wish you all the best and nothing less, and as always: here's to constructing YOU.

Printed in the USA
CPSIA information can be obtained
at www.ICGtesting.com
LVHW051257220524
780577LV00002B/177